Easy Everyday
FAVORITES
by MarkCharles Misilli

Author, MarkCharles Misilli. Special thanks to *Business Partners*, Steve Lichter and Lisa Matz. *Editors*, Jodi Flayman, Merly Mesa, Carol Ginsburg; *Recipe Development and Food Styling*, Patty Rosenthal; *Photographer*, Kelly Rusin; *Post Production*, Hal Silverman of Hal Silverman Studio; *Cover and Page Design*, Lorraine Dan of Grand Design

The paper in this printing meets the requirements of the ANSI Standard Z39.48-1992.

While every care has been taken in compiling the recipes for this book, the publisher, Cogin, Inc., or any other person who has been involved in working on this publication assumes no responsibility or liability for any errors or omissions, inadvertent or not, that may be found in the recipes or text, nor for any problems or damages that may arise as a result of preparing these recipes.

If food allergies or dietary restrictions are a concern, it is recommended that you carefully read ingredient product labels as well as consult a nutritionist or your physician to determine if a particular recipe meets your dietary needs.

We encourage you to use caution when working with all kitchen equipment and to always follow food safety guidelines.

To purchase this book for business or promotional use or to purchase more than 50 copies at a discount, or for custom editions, please contact Cogin, Inc. at the address below.

Inquiries should be addressed to:
Cogin, Inc.
1770 NW 64 Street, Suite 500
Fort Lauderdale, FL 33309

ISBN: 978-0-9911934-9-3

Printed in the United States of America
First Edition

FOREWORD

When it comes to making life easier in the kitchen...no one does it better than MarkCharles Misilli. In fact, he has dedicated his entire career to that goal. Known as the Gadget Guru on QVC, MarkCharles travels the globe looking for innovative ideas to make cooking and food preparation easier. So, when he decided to write a cookbook, I knew he would continue that same important mission.

Easy Everyday Favorites features delicious dishes that can all be made with common ingredients we keep in our kitchens on a regular basis. Home cooks like us are always in need of simple, tasty, and quick meals for our friends and families and this book delivers just that.

There are more than 130 delectable treats in this collection. Wait until you try yummy recipes such as: "Hotel Breakfast" Eggs Benedict, Crispy Fried Mac 'n' Cheese, Comforting Beef Barley Soup, Family-Sized Pizza Roll and Slow Cooker Apple Cobbler. From breakfast to casseroles to dessert, each page of this book shares clever, hearty, and fun dishes your family will ask for again and again. You'll also find plenty of color photos that give you wonderful direction on how the recipes should look and great ideas on presentation.

So, with life getting busier every day and time always running short, rest assured MarkCharles has your back. You can now come home and whip up perfect dishes for your family with ingredients you already have in the pantry and fridge. Not only will these meals get everyone around the dinner table, but they may also get a Happy Dance or two!

Keep it flavorful,

David Venable
QVC Host, In the Kitchen with David®

INTRODUCTION

Whether you know me from being a regular guest in the QVC kitchens for over 16 years, or you're simply looking for easy recipes to help make mealtime more exciting and life less stressful, then I know you're going to love this cookbook. Over my time at QVC, I've presented hundreds of kitchen products designed to make cooking quick, easy, and fun. Now, I'm excited to share with you a cookbook full of recipes that encompass that same philosophy.

The recipes are tried and true favorites that I grew up with, ones that I made for my kids while they grew up, or ones that I reach for whenever I need something quick. While I'm not a professional chef, I've always had a real passion for cooking. My love of cooking was gifted to me from one of the greatest cooks in the world—my meme (that's what I called my grandma). The weekends I spent in her kitchen are among my most cherished memories and it's where I learned how much fun you can have while cooking!

In this cookbook, I've included everything from rise and shine breakfast ideas to comforting dinner classics. Since I love to entertain, you'll also find plenty of party-special appetizers and bakery-worthy desserts. And unlike those other cookbooks that send you on a wild goose chase to find ingredients, every ingredient in this cookbook can easily be found at your local supermarket. Once you've got what you need, following the recipes is a cinch, since every one of them includes simple step-by-step instructions.

As you might imagine, I've got a pretty busy schedule. From being on QVC's "In the Kitchen with David" two days a week to all of the other responsibilities that come with what I do, you can bet that I don't have a whole lot of extra time to spend in the kitchen (I really wish I did!). I also know that I'm not the only busy person in the world...so are you. That's why I've included some of the best cooking tips and tricks that I've learned along the way. I guess you could say, I've done the grunt work, so you can just get in the kitchen and get it right the first time!

For all of you who picked up this cookbook because the cover made your mouth start to water, I've got good news. There are lots of full-page, color photos throughout the book. (Just when you thought it couldn't get any better, right?) I know that nothing tempts me more than seeing a larger than life version of my favorite sandwich (page 96). (Hey, I hope you really did turn to that page!)

So, whether you need to put dinner on the table for your family or you're planning on entertaining a few friends, you'll find that these recipes are exactly what you've been looking for. Before you go and get started, I want to thank you for trusting me all of these years with providing you the very best in kitchen gadgets, tips, and tricks—it really means a lot to me. I know that you and your family are going to love this book every bit as much as I did creating it for you. I look forward to hearing all about which recipes have become your new favorites.

MarkCharles Misilli

MY FAVORITE RECIPES

RECIPE

PAGE NUMBER

TABLE OF CONTENTS

Some days, I'm the guy that grabs a pastry and runs out the door. Other days, I've got the whole family sitting around the table waiting for a taste of my breakfast casserole. Whatever kind of day it is, I always make sure it starts off with something tasty. MCM

BREAKFAST & BRUNCH

FRENCH TOAST BRUNCH BAKE

Whenever I've got company coming over for brunch, I like to pull out all the stops. One way I do this is by making a variety of dishes. And although I usually like to change up my spread, the one dish that's always a staple is my French toast bake. It's the one that gets the most raves...probably because it tastes like dessert for breakfast!

Serves 6 to 8

1 (16-ounce) French bread, cut into 1-inch cubes (about 10 cups)

1 (8-ounce) package cream cheese, softened

8 eggs

1-½ cups milk

⅔ cup half-and-half

½ cup maple syrup

½ teaspoon ground cinnamon

1 teaspoon vanilla extract

2 tablespoons powdered sugar

■ Coat a 9- x 13-inch baking dish with cooking spray. Place bread cubes in baking dish.

■ In a large bowl, with an electric mixer, beat cream cheese until smooth. Add eggs one at a time, beating well after each addition. Add milk, half-and-half, maple syrup, cinnamon, and vanilla; mix until smooth.

■ Pour cream cheese mixture over bread cubes, cover, and chill at least 2 hours, or as long as overnight.

■ Preheat oven to 375 degrees F. Remove baking dish from refrigerator and let stand 20 minutes. Bake 45 to 50 minutes, or until set. Top with powdered sugar.

I usually serve this with some warm maple syrup, but when I make this for the holidays, I like to serve it with something a little extra-special, so I whip up a batch of homemade raspberry sauce. To make it, just combine 2 cups of fresh raspberries and ¼ cup of sugar in a saucepan. Let it cook for about 10 minutes, or until the raspberries break down. Then, stir in ½ a teaspoon of vanilla and it's ready to be enjoyed. MCM

TIRAMISU PANCAKE STACKS

If you're a fan of tiramisu with all of its layered, decadent goodness, then you're going to love this breakfast spin-off that trades ladyfingers for pancakes. I like to serve these hot off the griddle, so the creamy Italian filling melts between each layer. And when you finish each stack with a generous sprinkle of cocoa powder, you've made a breakfast that's restaurant-worthy.

Serves 8

1 (8-ounce) package cream cheese, softened

1 (8-ounce) container mascarpone cheese

⅔ cup powdered sugar

1 teaspoon instant coffee granules

2 tablespoons water

24 (4-inch) pancakes, made from pancake mix, following package directions

1 tablespoon unsweetened cocoa powder

■ In a large bowl, beat cream cheese, mascarpone cheese, and powdered sugar until well combined. In a small bowl, dissolve coffee granules in water, then add to cheese mixture; mix well. (This filling will last up to a week in the fridge or it can be frozen and used whenever you get a craving.)

■ Place a pancake on a plate, then dollop with cheese mixture; repeat layers two more times, ending with a dollop of cheese mixture topping the stack.

■ Repeat with remaining pancakes and cheese mixture. Sprinkle with cocoa and serve immediately.

If you don't have the time to cook up a batch of pancakes, feel free to use frozen ones. Just heat them according to package directions. MCM

SPECIAL MORNINGS STUFFED FRENCH TOAST

Some mornings I wake up with cravings for something really decadent, and on those mornings I make this lusciously creamy French toast. If you're a cheesecake lover, you're really going to love this recipe, because it's like getting to have your favorite dessert for breakfast. Let's just say, I never have any problem finding a few people to sit down and enjoy this dish with me.

Serves 4

3 ounces cream cheese, softened

2 tablespoons powdered sugar

2 tablespoons raspberry preserves

8 slices country white bread

2 eggs

½ cup half-and-half

2 tablespoons granulated sugar

4 tablespoons butter

■ In a small bowl, combine cream cheese and powdered sugar; mix well, then stir in preserves. Spread equally over 4 bread slices. Top with remaining bread slices, forming sandwiches.

■ In a shallow bowl, whisk eggs, half-and-half, and granulated sugar until well combined.

■ In a large skillet, melt 2 tablespoons butter over medium heat. Dip each sandwich into egg mixture, completely coating both sides. Cook 2 sandwiches at a time 1 to 2 minutes per side, or until golden. Melt remaining 2 tablespoons butter in skillet and cook remaining 2 sandwiches. Slice each in half diagonally, and serve.

For those really special mornings, you may want to top with a little more powdered sugar and some fresh fruit. MCM

BUTTERMILK BACON WAFFLES

When my kids were younger, getting them up and off to school was always sort of a challenge. But eventually, I found a trick that always got them out of bed a little earlier. All I had to do was tell them I was making their favorite buttermilk waffles studded with bacon. I'll never forget how they ran into the kitchen those mornings or how they liked to fill up each little square with syrup.

Makes 6

2 cups all-purpose flour

3 tablespoons sugar

1 teaspoon baking powder

1 teaspoon baking soda

½ teaspoon salt

2 eggs, beaten

2 cups buttermilk (see note)

4 tablespoons butter, melted

⅓ cup real bacon bits, finely chopped

- ■ Preheat a waffle iron according to directions. Coat with cooking spray.

- ■ In a large bowl, combine flour, sugar, baking powder, baking soda, and salt. Stir in eggs, buttermilk, melted butter, and bacon; mix well.

- ■ Using a ½-cup measure, pour batter onto bottom of prepared waffle iron. Close lid and cook 60 to 90 seconds, or until golden.

- ■ Using a fork, carefully remove waffle to a plate. Repeat with remaining batter. Serve immediately.

Whenever I'd forget to stock up on buttermilk, I would just make a quick and easy substitute. All you need to do is add 2 tablespoons of either white vinegar or cream of tartar to 2 cups of milk. Stir it all together and let it sit for about 5 minutes and voilà! You've got buttermilk to use in this recipe or any other recipe that calls for it. MCM

CHEESY EGG BUBBLE-UP BAKE

I just love how the biscuits in this breakfast dish "rise" to the occasion. The tops of the biscuits get all crusty and golden, while the eggs underneath stay light and fluffy. And all throughout, there's plenty of cheddar cheese to tie the two together. One time, when I made this for a brunch the day after a friend's wedding, I was told that it was, "like breakfast heaven in the form of a casserole."

Serves 6 to 8

1 (17.3-ounce) package refrigerated buttermilk biscuit dough (8 biscuits)

10 eggs

¼ cup milk

2 scallions, sliced

½ teaspoon salt

¼ teaspoon black pepper

1-¼ cups (5 ounces) shredded cheddar cheese, divided

■ Preheat oven to 375 degrees F. Coat a 2-½-quart casserole dish with cooking spray. Cut each biscuit into 6 pieces. (Believe it or not, one of the best way to cut these is with a pair of kitchen scissors.)

■ In a large bowl, whisk together the eggs, milk, scallions, salt, and pepper until well mixed. Stir ¾ cup of cheese into egg mixture. Add biscuit pieces and toss so that they all get their turn in the cheesy egg bath. Pour mixture into casserole dish.

■ Bake 45 minutes, or until center is set. Sprinkle on remaining cheese and continue to bake just until melted.

I am a big make-it-ahead kind of guy whenever possible, but this is one of those dishes that tastes best when it's straight out of the oven. MCM

GRAB 'N' GO OMELET MUFFINS

Most weeks, I've got a busy schedule to stick to. When I'm not on TV, I'm typically working on designing the next great kitchen gadget, attending business meetings, or running around town doing errands for myself and my kids. Instead of using those extra-busy days as an excuse to skip breakfast, I came up with these omelet muffins that I can make ahead of time and keep in the freezer for when I need to "grab-and-go."

Makes 6

5 eggs

½ cup chopped cooked ham

½ cup shredded Swiss cheese

¼ cup sliced scallions

A pinch of salt and pepper

■ Preheat oven to 350 degrees F. Coat 6 muffin cups with cooking spray. (Learn from my mistake, do not use paper liners for these since they will stick to the eggs. That's not the way we want to get our fiber!)

■ In a large bowl, beat the eggs until frothy. Add in the rest of the ingredients; mix well, then spoon evenly into the muffin cups.

■ Bake 20 to 25 minutes, or until eggs are set. Run a butter knife around the edge of each muffin cup and gently remove. Serve immediately or keep frozen until ready to warm in the microwave and enjoy.

"Hotel Breakfast" Eggs Benedict

If you haven't already guessed from the name of this recipe, this is what I refer to as my "hotel breakfast." It's the one thing I always order when I'm staying at a hotel and have time to enjoy it. If I'm making it at home it's typically for a special Sunday brunch or as a great way to toast the weekend. Either way, I know that if a morning starts with eggs Benedict, it's going to be a good day.

Serves 4

3 egg yolks

1 teaspoon Dijon mustard

1 tablespoon lemon juice

3 dashes hot pepper sauce

A pinch of salt

1 stick plus 1 tablespoon butter, divided

1 (6-ounce) package Canadian bacon

6 cups water

½ cup white vinegar

8 eggs

4 English muffins, split and toasted

Black pepper for sprinkling

Chives for sprinkling

■ In a blender, combine egg yolks, mustard, lemon juice, hot pepper sauce, and salt. Cover and blend 5 seconds; set aside.

■ In a microwave-safe bowl, melt 1 stick butter in microwave until melted and hot. Turn blender to high and slowly pour hot butter into yolk mixture; blend 5 to 10 seconds, or until thickened. (You've just made hollandaise sauce!) Place sauce in a bowl, then place in a bigger bowl of hot water to keep warm.

■ Meanwhile, in a large skillet over low heat, melt remaining 1 tablespoon butter; add Canadian bacon and cook 2 to 3 minutes per side, or until edges brown; set aside.

■ In another large skillet, bring water and vinegar to a boil. Crack eggs one at a time and gently drop each into boiling water. Cook 4 to 6 minutes, or until egg whites are firm and the yolks are to your liking.

■ Place a toasted English muffin on each plate and top each half with a slice of Canadian bacon. Using a slotted spoon, remove eggs from water and place one over each slice of bacon. Top eggs with hollandaise sauce, sprinkle with pepper and chives, and serve immediately.

CROISSANT BREAKFAST SANDWICH

There was no way I could get away without sharing one of my favorite French bakery pastries—the croissant. Nothing compares to fresh croissants in the morning, and if you've ever had the ones you bake up fresh from QVC, even better. While these buttery pastries are good on their own, whenever I'm really hungry I like to use them as the base of a breakfast sandwich. A few slices of tomato, fluffy scrambled eggs, and Havarti cheese make these perfect.

Makes 4

4 medium croissants

2 plum tomatoes, thinly sliced

4 eggs

1 tablespoon milk

A pinch of salt and pepper

1-½ teaspoons butter

4 slices Havarti cheese, cut in half diagonally

■ Preheat oven to 350 degrees F. Cut croissants in half lengthwise and place bottom halves on a baking sheet. Place 2 tomato slices evenly on each croissant bottom.

■ In a medium bowl, combine eggs, milk, salt, and pepper; mix well.

■ In a medium skillet over medium heat, melt butter; add egg mixture and scramble until firm, but not browned.

■ Spoon an equal amount of scrambled eggs onto each croissant bottom. Place a piece of cheese over the eggs and replace the top of each croissant. Place another piece of cheese over the top.

■ Bake 3 to 4 minutes, or until cheese is melted and sandwiches are heated through.

DOUBLE-CHEESE BROCCOLI QUICHE

Being a cheese lover sort of makes me a quiche lover too. (It's either that or it's my long line of French ancestry.) I just think it's great that there are so many ways to make it. For this quiche, I decided to showcase my love of cheese by using both a sharp cheddar and a mild and nutty Swiss. The broccoli is to make sure I get my greens in. Plus, who doesn't love the combination of broccoli and cheese?

Serves 6 to 8

1 cup (4 ounces) shredded cheddar cheese

1 cup (4 ounces) shredded Swiss cheese

1 (10-ounce) package frozen chopped broccoli, thawed and well drained

1 frozen ready-to-bake 9-inch pie shell, thawed

2 eggs

1 cup half-and-half

1 teaspoon onion powder

¼ teaspoon black pepper

¼ teaspoon ground nutmeg

■ Preheat oven to 350 degrees F.

■ In a medium bowl, combine cheddar cheese, Swiss cheese, and broccoli; mix well then spoon into pie shell.

■ In a small bowl, beat eggs, half-and-half, onion powder, and pepper until thoroughly combined. Pour into pie shell, then sprinkle with nutmeg.

■ Bake 40 to 45 minutes, or until firm and a toothpick inserted in center comes out clean. Let cool 5 minutes, then slice and serve.

You can make this a day or two before you plan to serve it. Cover and store it in the fridge, then slice when it's cold. You can reheat all of it in the oven or just a piece or two in the microwave when you're ready. MCM

EGG-IN-A-HOLE WITH ARUGULA SALAD

I love egg-in-a-hole. Some people might argue that it's for kids only, but I've found a way to elevate this childhood favorite into something that every adult will want to devour. Instead of traditional white bread, I like to use multigrain, and serve it with a side of arugula that's drizzled with a light Dijon vinaigrette. Trust me, it's the perfect way to kick off a great weekend.

Serves 2

½ cup olive oil

¼ cup red wine vinegar

2 tablespoons Dijon mustard

1 clove garlic, minced

1 teaspoon dried basil

½ teaspoon salt

¼ teaspoon black pepper

2 tablespoons lemon juice

4 slices multigrain bread

2 tablespoons butter, softened

4 eggs

Salt and pepper to taste

Sriracha sauce (optional)

2 cups fresh arugula

■ To make dressing, in a small bowl, whisk oil, vinegar, mustard, garlic, basil, ½ teaspoon salt, and ¼ teaspoon pepper. Add lemon juice and whisk until thoroughly combined; set aside.

■ Cut a 2-inch hole in each slice of bread; evenly butter both sides. In a griddle pan or large skillet over medium heat, toast one side of buttered bread 2 to 3 minutes, or until golden. Flip bread over, then crack an egg into each hole. Cook eggs to desired doneness. Sprinkle with salt and pepper and a little sriracha sauce, if you want a kick.

■ Serve arugula on the side, drizzled with dressing.

You'll have some extra dressing, so you can serve it on the side or keep it in the fridge for up to a week in a cruet. If you have one of these, you'll know why I love it so much! MCM

ALL-IN-ONE BREAKFAST CASSEROLE

I've been to a lot of diners throughout the years, and I can tell you that the one thing they all have in common is the combo platter that comes loaded with eggs, hash browns, and some kind of breakfast meat. It's practically as popular as butter on toast! That's why I thought it'd be a great idea to make a casserole that bakes them all together. Now, you get a little bit of everything in every forkful.

Serves 6 to 8

1 pound hot or mild ground pork sausage

½ (16-ounce) package frozen shredded hash brown potatoes (about 3 cups)

1 cup (4 ounces) shredded sharp cheddar cheese

6 eggs, beaten

¾ cup milk

¾ teaspoon dry mustard

½ teaspoon salt

A pinch of black pepper

■ Preheat oven to 350 degrees F. Coat a 9- x 13-inch baking dish with cooking spray.

■ In a large skillet over medium-high heat, brown sausage, stirring until it crumbles and is no longer pink; drain. Layer potatoes, sausage, and cheese in baking dish.

■ In a medium bowl, combine remaining ingredients; pour over cheese.

■ Bake, covered, 30 minutes; uncover and bake an additional 5 minutes, or until set. Let stand 10 minutes before serving.

If you prefer to get a jump-start on breakfast, this is a great make-ahead recipe. Just assemble all the ingredients, as instructed, then cover and place in the fridge overnight. When you're ready to eat, all you have to do is bake this off and you're all set! MCM

1-MINUTE PIZZA SCRAMBLE

There are a lot of people who will eat cold, leftover pizza for breakfast when they don't have a lot of time or just don't know what else to make. I know I've done it! Hopefully, this recipe will change that. In just about the same amount of time as it takes for you to read the rest of this page, you can whip up a scrambled egg pizza bowl in your microwave.

Serves 1

2 eggs

2 tablespoons chopped pepperoni

2 tablespoons milk

A pinch of salt and pepper

2 tablespoons shredded mozzarella cheese

■ Coat a microwave-safe cereal bowl with cooking spray. Add eggs, pepperoni, milk, salt, and pepper; beat until well blended.

■ Microwave 45 seconds; stir. Top with cheese and microwave 30 to 45 more seconds, or until eggs are set. Serve immediately.

Add some of your favorite chopped veggies, like bell peppers, onions, or mushrooms for colorful, flavorful, and healthy additions to your scramble! MCM

APRICOT AND CHEESE DANISH PASTRIES

Whenever I get a little "me-time," which these days is pretty rare, I like to make myself a cup of coffee and sit down with a creamy, cheesy pastry. Some days I'm lucky enough to get this in first thing in the morning, while other days I can't find a break until much later in the day. That's what's so nice about these—you can enjoy them any time you want.

Serves 12 to 15

⅓ cup chopped walnuts

¾ cup sugar, divided

½ teaspoon ground cinnamon

2 (8-ounce) cans refrigerated crescent roll dough

12 ounces cream cheese, softened

1 teaspoon vanilla extract

½ cup apricot preserves

2 tablespoons butter, melted

■ Preheat oven to 350 degrees F. In a small bowl, combine walnuts, ¼ cup sugar, and the cinnamon; set aside. Unroll 1 can of crescent dough and press into bottom of a 9- x 13-inch baking dish, pressing seams together.

■ In a large bowl, combine cream cheese, the remaining ½ cup sugar, and vanilla; mix well. Carefully spread cream cheese mixture over dough, then gently spread apricot preserves over cream cheese mixture. (If you want to try these with another preserve flavor, like pineapple or raspberry, go for it.)

■ Unroll remaining can of dough and place over apricot preserves. Pour butter evenly over dough and sprinkle with nut mixture.

■ Bake 20 to 25 minutes, or until golden brown. Let cool before cutting. Refrigerate leftovers.

SOUTHERN COMFORT SAUSAGE AND BISCUITS

I didn't grow up eating Southern foods, but when I finally got the chance to taste some real down-home Southern cooking, I understood why everyone raves about it. This dish just shouts comfort to me. It's the kind of breakfast that I would serve to someone who needs a little warming up, because it's almost like giving them a hug from the inside-out. Between the freshly baked biscuits and the homemade country-style gravy, you just can't go wrong.

Serves 4 to 6

1 (17.3-ounce) package refrigerated buttermilk biscuit dough (8 biscuits)

1 (16-ounce) tube hot pork sausage

1 small onion, chopped

3 tablespoons all-purpose flour

1 teaspoon Worcestershire sauce

2 cups milk

¼ teaspoon salt

¼ teaspoon black pepper

■ Bake biscuits according to package directions; set aside.

■ Meanwhile, in a large skillet over medium-high heat, cook sausage and onion 6 to 8 minutes, or until no pink remains in the sausage, stirring to crumble the meat. (Make sure to use the hot pork sausage that comes in a tube, not the hot Italian pork sausage that comes from the meat case.) Add flour; mix well. Add Worcestershire sauce, milk, salt, and pepper; mix well.

■ Cook 2 to 3 additional minutes, or until gravy thickens, stirring constantly. Serve over biscuits.

I sometimes like to add chopped chives for a little color and an extra spark of flavor.

MCM

HEARTY HELPINGS HASH BROWN SKILLET

I'll admit it, I'm not a pepper lover. There, I said it and I feel better. So, one morning I was making hash browns for a friend of mine who loves everything and anything with peppers and onions and I decided to surprise her by adding them to the batch I had on the stove. I'll never forget how excited she was to see that I put her love for peppers over my personal tastes. You should've seen her chow down on this!

Serves 4 to 6

¼ cup olive oil

1 (2-pound) package frozen diced hash brown potatoes

1 red bell pepper, chopped

1 onion, chopped

2 cups sliced fresh mushrooms

1 teaspoon salt

½ teaspoon black pepper

2 cups fresh spinach

■ In a large skillet over high heat, heat oil until hot.

■ Add potatoes and cook 10 to 12 minutes, or until lightly browned. Add bell pepper, onion, mushrooms, salt, and pepper. Cook 6 to 8 additional minutes, or until vegetables are tender, stirring occasionally. Add spinach and cook 1 more minute. Serve immediately.

NO-FUSS STICKY BUNS

There's nothing fussy about these sticky buns, which makes them a great option for a busy weekday breakfast (or dessert!). I like that they're a little sticky and a lot gooey, but also have a bit of crunch to them thanks to all the pecans. I think these are best when they're served fresh from the oven, and washed down with a big glass of milk. Just don't forget to set out the napkins—you're going to need them!

Makes 9

½ cup packed light brown sugar, divided

3 tablespoons butter, melted, divided

1 tablespoon light corn syrup

¾ cup chopped pecans, divided

1 (8-ounce) package refrigerated crescent roll dough

1 teaspoon ground cinnamon

- Preheat oven to 375 degrees F. Coat an 8-inch square baking dish with cooking spray.

- In a small bowl, combine ¼ cup brown sugar, 2 tablespoons butter, and the corn syrup; mix until smooth, then spread over bottom of baking dish. Sprinkle with ½ cup pecans.

- Unroll crescent dough and press seams together to form one large rectangle. Brush with remaining tablespoon butter. Sprinkle with remaining ¼ cup brown sugar, the cinnamon, and the remaining ¼ cup pecans.

- Starting at the wide end, roll up dough jelly roll-style. With a sharp knife, cut into 9 equal slices and place each slice cut-side down in baking dish.

- Bake 18 to 20 minutes, or until puffed and golden. Remove from oven and immediately invert onto serving platter. Allow to cool slightly, then serve warm.

BLUEBERRY BANANA SMOOTHIE

This is one of my favorite go-to smoothies. It's pretty basic, but the combination of blueberries and bananas just works so well together and the yogurt makes it extra-creamy. It's not just for breakfast either—I make it whenever I need a sweet and healthy pick-me-up, like before I go on-air with David.

Serves 2-3

2 large ripe bananas, sliced

1 cup blueberries, frozen or fresh

1 cup low-fat Greek vanilla yogurt

3 cups ice cubes

■ In a blender, combine bananas, blueberries, and yogurt until smooth.

■ Add ice cubes and blend until crushed and well combined. Pour into glasses and serve immediately.

SUMMER-FRESH SMOOTHIE

In the summer, when strawberries and mangoes are extra sweet, I like to eat them every which way I can. Somehow, I always end up with more than even I can eat, so I just cut them up and pop them in the freezer. Then, I can use my frozen fruit pieces to make fresh-tasting smoothies all year long. It's simple, sweet, and so satisfying.

Serves 2-3

1 cup fresh strawberries

1 banana

1 ripe mango

¼ cup orange juice

½ cup vanilla yogurt

2 tablespoons honey

1 cup ice cubes

■ Wash and hull the strawberries. Cut banana into chunks. Pit, peel, and slice the mango.

■ In a blender, combine all ingredients; blend until smooth. Pour into glasses and serve immediately.

COFFEEHOUSE MOCHA FRAPPÉ

Some people are coffee people and some people are tea people. I'm a coffee person. And while I'm perfectly okay with a regular cup of joe, I do like to splurge on fancy coffeehouse drinks from time to time. Luckily, I found a way to keep some money in my pocket and still enjoy that gourmet taste right at home. I've got to tell you, it's so simple you'll wish you'd tried it sooner.

Serves 1

1 cup milk

¼ cup chocolate syrup

¼ cup instant
coffee granules

⅓ cup sugar

1 (1.26-ounce) envelope
vanilla instant
breakfast drink mix

¼ teaspoon
almond extract

3 cups ice cubes

■ In a blender, blend all ingredients except ice, until well combined.

■ Add ice and blend until well combined and slushy. Serve immediately.

This is the chapter that's going to have you dipping, dunking, grabbing, popping, pulling, and digging for more. Whether you serve these at a party or before a family dinner, they're going to make you look good! MCM

STARTERS

CRISPY-FRIED MAC & CHEESE

If you didn't look at these and experience what I like to call "jaw-dropping wonder," then I don't know what else to say to you. I can think of a hundred reasons to make these, which is why I sometimes refer to them as "anytizers." I've eaten them as a snack, made them to celebrate a championship win with my kid's team, and even served them at a cocktail party. I can promise you, they've been a hit every time.

Makes about 25

1 (20-ounce) package frozen macaroni and cheese, thawed

1 egg

1 tablespoon water

1-½ cups panko bread crumbs

½ teaspoon paprika

¼ teaspoon garlic powder

¼ teaspoon salt

A pinch of black pepper

A pinch of ground red pepper (optional)

1-½ cups vegetable oil

■ Using a heaping teaspoon or small ice cream scoop, form macaroni and cheese into 1-inch balls and place on a wax paper-lined baking sheet. They don't need to be perfectly shaped, but you do want them packed firmly so they hold together. Freeze 2 hours, or until firm.

■ Meanwhile, in a shallow dish, beat egg and water. In another shallow dish, combine bread crumbs, paprika, garlic powder, salt, and pepper. If you like a little heat, you'll add the pinch of ground red pepper, too.

■ In a deep saucepan over medium heat, heat oil until hot (about 350 degrees F).

■ Dip frozen macaroni balls into egg mixture, then roll in the seasoned bread crumbs. In small batches, fry balls 3 to 5 minutes, or until they become golden and the center is hot. Keep remaining macaroni balls frozen until ready to fry. Drain on a paper towel-lined tray and serve immediately, or keep refrigerated until ready to serve.

I like to make these a day or two before serving them. Then, all I have to do is take them out of the fridge, place them on a baking sheet, and rewarm them in a 300-degree oven for about 10 minutes. MCM

CHEESY BACON DROPS

You really can't go wrong with something that's basically a little puff loaded with cheese and bacon, but if you want to go all-out you have to serve these with a bunch of different sauces. I've been known to set up a sauce buffet to go alongside them. Some of my offerings include wing sauce, ranch, blue cheese, honey mustard, and even a gooey cheese dip for my die-hard cheese fans. I've found that people are really into mixing and matching.

Makes about 36

1 cup milk

½ stick butter

1 cup all-purpose flour

4 eggs

8 slices bacon, cooked crisp and crumbled

⅓ cup thinly sliced scallion

1 cup shredded Mexican cheese blend

¾ teaspoon salt

■ Preheat oven to 350 degrees F. Coat 2 baking sheets with cooking spray.

■ In a medium saucepan over medium heat, combine milk and butter and heat until butter is melted and mixture is hot. Add flour and use a wooden spoon to stir these like crazy, until mixture forms a ball, then remove from heat.

■ Stir in 1 egg at a time until mixture is smooth. Repeat with remaining eggs, until thoroughly combined. Stir in bacon, scallions, cheese and salt. Drop mixture by teaspoonfuls onto prepared baking sheets.

■ Bake 15 to 18 minutes, or until they've puffed up and turned golden. Serve these piping hot, right from the oven, or keep them in the fridge a day or two and warm them when you get a last-minute call from your friends saying they're just around the corner.

TAKE-OUT EGG ROLLS

Don't be that person who orders take-out for the party! Instead, be the person who surprises everyone by starting off the party with a tray of crispy, homemade egg rolls. There's a good chance you're probably thinking, "But I can't make those! They're too complicated." Here's the good news—they're not. My version is simple and freakin' delicious. Serve them up with a little duck sauce and hot mustard and bask in your awesomeness.

Makes 12

¼ cup packed brown sugar

½ cup soy sauce

1 tablespoon ground ginger

2 teaspoons garlic powder

6 cups finely shredded Chinese (Napa) cabbage

1 carrot, shredded

3 scallions, thinly sliced

1 cup diced cooked chicken

12 egg roll wrappers

1 egg, lightly beaten

Vegetable or peanut oil for frying

■ In a small bowl, combine brown sugar, soy sauce, ginger, and garlic powder; mix well.

■ In a large bowl, combine cabbage, carrot, scallions, and chicken; mix well. Pour soy sauce mixture over cabbage mixture; toss to coat well and let marinate for about 10 minutes. Place cabbage mixture in a colander and squeeze to drain well. Don't skip this step or you'll end up with soggy eggrolls.

■ Spoon about ½ cup cabbage mixture evenly onto center of each egg roll wrapper. Lightly brush edges of egg roll with beaten egg. Fold one corner of each egg roll wrapper over the cabbage mixture, sort of tucking the point under the filling with your fingers. Then, firmly fold both sides of the wrapper over the filling and roll up tightly.

■ In a deep medium saucepan over medium-high heat, heat about 1-½ inches oil until hot. Add egg rolls in batches and fry 3 to 4 minutes per side, or until golden. Drain on a cooling rack. Serve immediately, and be careful—the filling will be hot.

Sometimes I like to make mini egg rolls. To do that, I just use wonton wrappers instead of egg roll wrappers. For the mini kind, put in about a tablespoon of filling in each. You should end up with about 48 of these. MCM

REALLY MESSY CHICKEN WINGS

Wings are the ultimate game day food. As long as there are wings, a few cases of beer, and like, five different options for chips and dip, most people are satisfied. For these, you might want to give every guest their own roll of paper towels, because they're covered in a really sticky-sweet sauce. Either that, or you can just sit back and watch them go to town licking their fingers. Hey, it's up to you!

Serves 6 to 8

4 pounds split chicken wings or drumettes, thawed if frozen

1 cup sweet and sour sauce

½ cup honey

¼ cup Thai sweet chili sauce

1 tablespoon soy sauce

3 cloves garlic, chopped

1 teaspoon ground ginger

■ Preheat oven to 425 degrees F. Line a 10- x 15-inch rimmed baking sheet with aluminum foil. Place wings in a single layer—this will help them crisp up. Bake 30 minutes; drain excess liquid.

■ In a large bowl, combine remaining ingredients; mix well. Set aside ½ cup mixture.

■ Place the wings in the large bowl with the sauce and toss until evenly coated; return to baking sheet.

■ Bake an additional 25 to 30 minutes, or until sauce begins to caramelize and wings are crispy. Toss wings in reserved mixture and serve immediately.

MASHED POTATO PUFF BALLS

One potato, two potato, three potato, four... How many of these potato balls do you think you'll eat before your guests arrive? I won't even admit how many I ate the first time I made them. This recipe is for anyone who has ever dreamed of eating mashed potatoes with their hands, but was told it wasn't socially acceptable. Guess what naysayers? These are a party favorite!

Makes about 72

3 pounds russet potatoes, peeled and quartered

3 tablespoons olive oil

1 large onion, chopped

1 cup bread or cornflake crumbs

2 teaspoons salt

½ teaspoon black pepper

2 egg yolks, beaten

■ Place potatoes in a soup pot and add just enough water to cover them. Bring to a boil over high heat, then reduce heat to medium and cook 12 to 15 minutes, or until fork-tender. Drain off water, mash the potatoes, and allow to cool slightly.

■ Meanwhile, in a small saucepan over medium heat, heat oil until hot, but not smoking; add onion and sauté until tender.

■ Add sauteéd onion, bread crumbs, salt, and pepper to mashed potatoes; mix well.

■ Preheat oven to 400 degrees F. Coat 2 baking sheets with cooking spray.

■ Using your hands, roll mixture into 1-½-inch balls and place on baking sheets. Brush with egg yolk and bake 40 to 45 minutes, or until golden.

To change these up at times, I have added a ¼ cup or so of crumbled bacon to the potatoes before rolling them. It gives them a smoky flavor that's really tasty. MCM

JUST-FOR-YOU STUFFED MUSHROOMS

Here's something you may not know about me: I'm allergic to mushrooms. But even though I can't eat them, that doesn't mean I won't make them for my friends and family. It took a lot of back-and-forth with my taste-testers on this one, but they finally said this was the best combination I had ever come up with. It's basically French onion soup stuffed inside a mushroom. I even made sure to include the best part—a layer of cheese on top!

Makes 12

1 pound large fresh mushrooms

3 tablespoons butter

½ cup finely chopped onion

1 packet onion soup mix

1 tablespoon water

¼ cup plain bread crumbs

A pinch of black pepper

3 slices Swiss cheese, each slice cut into 4 squares

■ Preheat oven to 375 degrees F. Gently clean mushrooms by wiping them with damp paper towels. Don't wash them or they'll turn mushy. Remove stems from 12 mushrooms; set aside caps. Finely chop mushroom stems and any remaining whole mushrooms.

■ In a large skillet over medium heat, melt butter; cook onion 3 minutes, or just until soft. Stir in chopped mushrooms, onion soup mix, and water and cook 4 to 5 minutes, or until tender. If you want, you can add a splash of red wine in place of the water for a fancier taste. Remove from heat and stir in bread crumbs and black pepper.

■ Using a teaspoon, stuff each mushroom cap with stuffing. Place on an ungreased baking sheet.

■ Bake 12 minutes. Remove from oven, top each with a piece of cheese, and return to oven for 5 minutes, or until cheese is melted and mushrooms are heated through. Serve immediately.

PARTY-TIME DEVILED EGGS

It's not a coincidence that you always see deviled eggs served at parties. Everyone knows they're good and they're pretty easy to make (especially if you have my Eggspress Egg Cooker and Poacher). There are lots of different ways to make them, but I don't think you can beat the classic combination of mayo, mustard, sweet relish, and a finishing touch of paprika. Hmm, it might be time to throw another party soon...

Makes 12

6 hard-boiled eggs, peeled and cut in half lengthwise

½ cup mayonnaise

2 teaspoons mustard

2 tablespoons sweet relish, drained

Paprika for sprinkling

■ In a small bowl, mash egg yolks and combine with mayonnaise, mustard and relish; mix well. (If you feel strongly for another kind of mustard, like a Dijon or spicy brown mustard, go ahead and make the swap.)

■ Fill egg white halves with yolk mixture and place on a platter. You can do this with a spoon or a pastry bag, if you have one. Sprinkle each egg with a little paprika. Cover with plastic wrap and refrigerate until ready to serve.

SOUTH PACIFIC SLOW COOKER MEATBALLS

Slow cookers are like magic kitchen wizards. They not only take half the work out of cooking, but they also make things taste so amazingly good. Take these meatballs, for instance. All you have to do is dump in all of the ingredients, set the slow cooker to start doing its thing, and, hours later, they're ready to be devoured. Did I mention how great your house is going to smell?

Serves 10 to 14

1-¼ cups sweet and sour sauce

¼ cup light brown sugar

3 tablespoons soy sauce

½ teaspoon garlic powder

½ teaspoon black pepper

2-½ pounds frozen cocktail-size meatballs

1 red bell pepper, chopped

1 (20-ounce) can pineapple chunks, drained

■ Place all ingredients in a 5-quart slow cooker; stir gently, then cover with lid. (The nice thing about this recipe is that it's so adaptable. When fresh mangos are available, I like to cut them up and add them in, and if you don't have light brown sugar, you can use dark brown sugar for a richer flavor.)

■ Cook on LOW 7 to 8 hours, or on HIGH 4 to 5 hours, or until heated through.

■ Carefully remove lid to allow steam to escape. Serve directly from slow cooker.

Instead of serving these with toothpicks or cocktail forks, I like to have a little fun and put out a bowl of pretzel sticks. They make a great edible alternative! MCM

CREAMY SPINACH PINWHEELS

To all my friends and family who have casually decided to "drop by" without warning over the years, this recipe is a result of the anxiety you caused me. (Thank you.) No really, I needed to come up with a quick appetizer that required no cooking and would still impress you all. This creamy spinach pinwheel, stuffed with bacon bits and pimientos, was the result. The maybe-bad news is, I think it's caused more of you to drop by unexpectedly.

Makes 40

1 (8-ounce) package cream cheese, softened

¾ cup mayonnaise

½ cup grated Parmesan cheese

½ teaspoon garlic powder

1 teaspoon lemon juice

1 (10-ounce) package frozen chopped spinach, thawed and drained well

2 (2-ounce) jars diced pimientos, drained well

1 (3-ounce) package bacon bits

5 (10-inch) flour tortillas

■ In a large bowl, combine cream cheese, mayonnaise, Parmesan cheese, garlic powder, and lemon juice; mix well. Stir in spinach, pimientos, and bacon bits.

■ Spread mixture on tortillas, distributing evenly. Roll up jellyroll fashion; wrap each in plastic wrap.

■ Chill 1 to 2 hours, or until ready to serve. Cut into 1-inch thick slices and serve.

You can make these a little healthier by swapping out the flour tortillas for the whole wheat kind and using reduced fat versions of the cream cheese and mayo. Just making these changes will cut out a lot of the fat. MCM

CHEESE-STUFFED ITALIAN MEATBALLS

Like any good half-Italian, I grew up eating meatballs every Sunday. A true Italian will tell you that there are no shortcuts when it comes to making meatballs, which is why I completely embrace all parts of me and say, "Go for the shortcuts!" Nowadays, there are so many great jarred sauces that taste just like homemade. Your guests probably won't notice, especially once they see the cheese oozing out of the meatballs.

Makes 20

½ pound ground pork

½ pound ground beef

½ cup Italian
bread crumbs

½ cup grated
Parmesan cheese

½ cup water

1 teaspoon Italian
seasoning

1 egg

1-½ teaspoons
garlic powder

½ teaspoon salt

¾ teaspoon black pepper

1 (8-ounce) package
mozzarella cheese, cut
into 20 (½-inch) cubes

1 (24-ounce) jar
spaghetti sauce

■ Preheat oven to 350 degrees F. Coat a baking sheet with cooking spray.

■ In a large bowl, combine all ingredients except mozzarella cheese and spaghetti sauce; mix well.

■ Form mixture into 20 (1-½-inch) meatballs, then form each meatball around a cheese cube, making sure to cover cheese completely. Make sure the mozzarella cheese is cold before you form your meatball around it. If not, it may ooze out while baking. Place on baking sheet. Bake 15 to 20 minutes, or until meat is no longer pink.

■ In a large saucepan over medium-low heat, heat spaghetti sauce until hot. Add meatballs, toss until evenly coated, and simmer for a couple of minutes before serving.

SOUTHWESTERN CORN CAKES

Traditionally, corn cakes are served with warm maple syrup poured all over them, but I wanted to break from tradition and share a recipe that's going to have your whole family saying, "Yeehaw!" Okay, maybe not... One thing's for sure, they're going to love these bite-sized, cowboy-inspired corn cakes.

Makes about 24

1-¾ cups all-purpose flour

2 teaspoons
baking powder

1 teaspoon salt

½ teaspoon black pepper

2 eggs, beaten

¼ cup salsa

1 (14-¾-ounce) can
cream-style corn

1 cup frozen corn, thawed

¼ cup vegetable oil,
or more as needed

■ In a large bowl, combine flour, baking powder, salt, and pepper. Add eggs and salsa; mix well. Stir in both corns. (As for the salsa, you can use mild, medium, or hot based on what you like best.)

■ In a large skillet over medium heat, heat 1 tablespoon oil until hot, but not smoking. Drop batter into hot skillet 1 tablespoonful at a time and cook 4 to 5 minutes, or until golden, turning corn cakes halfway through cooking. Remove to a paper towel-lined platter.

■ Add another tablespoon oil to skillet. When hot, repeat with remaining batter, adding more oil as needed, until all batter is used.

SEASIDE CRAB CAKES

So, you want to serve an authentic dockside favorite? Now, you can go ahead and get the lobster prepped and buttered OR you can just let everyone enjoy a few of these crab cakes. (I like to go for option B—it's much easier on my pocket!) These crab cakes will take your taste buds on a trip to that seaside town you've always dreamt about.

Makes 18

1 egg

½ cup mayonnaise

1 tablespoon Dijon mustard

1 tablespoon hot sauce

2 cloves garlic, minced

½ teaspoon salt

¼ teaspoon black pepper

¾ cup bread crumbs

1 pound lump crab meat

4 tablespoons vegetable oil

■ In a large bowl, whisk together egg, mayonnaise, mustard, hot sauce, garlic, salt, and pepper. Gently stir in bread crumbs and crab meat until just combined. (You can use crab claw meat instead of lump crab meat, since it's much cheaper.) Make sure not to overmix or you'll ruin the tender, flaky consistency.

■ Form into 18 mini crab cakes and place on a wax paper-lined platter. Refrigerate 30 minutes. Doing this helps them retain their shape while cooking.

■ In a large skillet over medium heat, heat 2 tablespoons oil until hot, but not smoking. Sauté crab cakes 4 to 6 minutes per side, or until golden brown. Remove to a platter and cover with foil to keep warm. Repeat with remaining crab cakes.

Typically, I serve these as hors d'oeuvres, but if you'd rather make them for lunch or dinner, I find that they can be formed into about 6 larger crab cakes, and cooked just a bit longer. MCM

TACO TUESDAY TOTCHOS

2-22-20
Pretty Good

I'm glad that Taco Tuesday is such a big thing now. It's an excuse for me to go out, on a Tuesday, and stuff my face with all kinds of Mexican food. My kids are really into it too, so a lot of times we make it a family trip or just do our own version at home. This recipe is a great spin-off of that idea. The only not-so-great part about it is that they're usually gone before I can get my share!

Serves 6 to 8

1 (28-ounce) package frozen potato tots

1 pound ground beef

1 (1-¼-ounce) package taco seasoning mix

¼ cup water

2 cups shredded Colby Jack cheese

1 (2-¼-ounce) can sliced black olives, drained

1 jalapeño, thinly sliced

1 cup fresh salsa

1 ripe avocado, cut into 1-inch chunks

½ cup sour cream (optional)

■ Preheat oven to 400 degrees F. Coat a baking sheet with cooking spray. Place potato tots in a single layer on baking sheet and bake 25 to 30 minutes, or until crispy. If you like your tots extra crispy, coat them with cooking spray before baking.

■ Meanwhile, in a large skillet over medium-high heat, brown beef 6 to 8 minutes, or until no pink remains, stirring occasionally to crumble; drain excess liquid. I like to stir and crumble the meat with a potato masher to make sure it's well crumbled. Stir in taco seasoning and water. Cook 2 to 4 minutes, or until heated through.

■ Spoon beef mixture over potato tots, then top with cheese, olives, and jalapeño slices. Return to oven 4 to 5 minutes, or until cheese is melted. Top with salsa, avocado, and sour cream, if desired, before serving.

OOEY GOOEY CHEESE BREAD

I'll admit it—this is so good I've eaten the leftovers cold, right out of the fridge. (Don't judge me until you've tasted it yourself!) I know that garlic bread is usually the most popular choice, but that's because most people haven't been introduced to this mouthwatering, creamy, cheesy, 5-ingredient-easy, loaf of pure deliciousness...You know what? I think you need to make this right now.

Serves 6 to 8

1 (8-ounce) package cream cheese, softened

2 tablespoons mayonnaise

1 (1-ounce) packet ranch dressing mix

1 large French baguette

1 (8-ounce) package shredded four cheese mix

■ Preheat oven to 350 degrees F. Line a baking sheet with aluminum foil.

■ In a medium bowl, mix together cream cheese, mayonnaise, and dressing mix; set aside.

■ Cut bread in half lengthwise and place both halves, cut-side-up, on a baking sheet. I like to use a French baguette, but you can also make this with an Italian bread or a crusty loaf of sourdough.

■ Spread cream cheese mixture evenly over both cut sides. Sprinkle shredded cheese evenly over the cream cheese spread. Place on prepared baking sheet.

■ Bake 10 to 15 minutes, or until the topping is golden and melty. Place on a cutting board, slice and serve.

Since this bread is so easy and takes less than 15 minutes from start to finish, I usually make this as a last-minute appetizer, but you can also serve it alongside hearty main dishes, like ribs or meatloaf. Trust me on this one; people are going to love it no matter when it makes an appearance. MCM

TABLESIDE GUACAMOLE

At one of my favorite Mexican restaurants in town you can actually ask for your guacamole to be made tableside. The server will come to your table with all the ingredients and mash it in front of you, so you know it's extra-fresh. I love this idea, so I came up with this super-simple, 5-ingredient guacamole recipe that you can put together right at the table for your family and friends.

Makes 2 cups

3 large ripe avocados

¼ cup salsa

1 tablespoon fresh lemon juice

¼ teaspoon garlic powder

¼ teaspoon salt

■ In a medium bowl, mash the avocados with a fork until chunky. (It's important that you use a ripe avocado or you'll end up with tasteless guacamole.)

■ Add remaining ingredients; mix well. (I usually make this with mild salsa, but feel free to use medium or hot, if you prefer.) Serve, or cover and chill until ready to serve.

Make your own crispy Lime & Sea Salt Tortilla Chips! All you need to do is place 2 cups of water mixed with 2 tablespoons of lime juice in a pie plate. Dip 6 tortillas, one at a time, into the water for a couple of seconds each. Then, cut each into 8 wedges. Lay them out in a single layer on a baking sheet that's been coated with cooking spray. Sprinkle lightly with sea salt and bake 5 to 8 minutes, or until they're crispy. MCM

7-LAYER GREEK DIP

I'm hoping you've got more self-control than me because every time I make this 7-layer dip, I have a hard time not hovering around it. I just want to keep going in, one pita chip at a time! Honestly, if you love Greek food as much as my family does, then get ready to become obsessed with this dip. It's basically all of our favorite Greek restaurant ingredients in one tasty dip.

Serves 8 to 10

2 (8-ounce) containers hummus

1 cup plain Greek yogurt

1 tomato, diced

1 cup diced cucumber

½ cup diced roasted peppers, drained well

½ cup crumbled feta cheese

½ cup chopped pitted Kalamata olives

½ teaspoon dried oregano

⅛ teaspoon black pepper

1 tablespoon lemon juice

■ Evenly spread hummus on a platter. Dollop yogurt over hummus and spread gently. Sprinkle with tomato, cucumber, red peppers, feta cheese, and olives. Sprinkle with oregano and black pepper. Drizzle with lemon juice.

■ Serve immediately or refrigerate until ready to serve.

This feeds a crowd, so make sure you have plenty of fresh cut veggies and pita wedges to serve this with. You can also do as I did and set out a few bottles of Pinot Grigio. One of my guests told me she spent the rest of the day dreaming about traveling to the Mediterranean! MCM

HAM SALAD CRACKER SPREAD

Break out a few cracker sleeves, get out your cheese board, and set out some rye bread because this ham salad is going to help you get your party started. An all-American favorite, my recipe is an updated version of the one your grandma used to make. By making some simple changes, like adding cheddar cheese and swapping out traditional yellow mustard for a spicy brown mustard, this spread becomes trendy again.

Makes 2-½ cups

2 cups cooked ham, cut into chunks

¾ cup shredded cheddar cheese

⅓ cup chopped onion

¼ cup sweet pickle relish, drained

½ cup mayonnaise

1 tablespoon spicy brown mustard

¼ teaspoon black pepper

■ Place all ingredients in a food processor fitted with its cutting blade. Process on medium speed 1 minute. Scrape down the sides of the bowl with a rubber spatula and process for another minute until everything is thoroughly combined.

■ Chill for at least one hour before serving.

If you've got one of my Pull Chop Food Choppers this recipe is a great one to use it on! The great thing about it is, you can make it as chunky or as fine as you like. MCM

I'm not a huge rule follower, that's why I love making soups and salads. It's so easy to get creative; a little bit of this, a little of that and voilà! You've got yourself a new creation. MCM

SOUP & SALAD

CREAMY BROCCOLI-CHEDDAR SOUP

Look, some dishes just aren't meant to be light. Every once in a while, you've got to let yourself enjoy a hearty and creamy soup that's probably not going to help trim your waistline. It's okay! There's lots of butter, cheese, and cream in this recipe and it's what makes it taste so amazing (oh yeah, the broccoli, too!). Every spoonful is like a reward, and whatever I can't pick up with my spoon, I just go ahead and soak up with crusty bread.

Serves 4 to 6

2 heads broccoli,
trimmed and chopped

½ cup chopped onion

1 teaspoon black pepper

5 cups chicken broth

1 stick butter

½ cup all-purpose flour

1 cup (½ pint) half-and-half

3 cups (12 ounces)
shredded cheddar cheese

■ In a soup pot over high heat, combine broccoli, onion, pepper, and broth; bring to a boil. Reduce heat to low, cover, and simmer about 30 minutes, or until the broccoli is tender.

■ Meanwhile, in a skillet over medium heat, melt butter; slowly whisk in flour, stirring continuously until golden. (This is what is called a roux and will thicken the soup.)

■ Slowly add the butter mixture (roux) to the soup, stirring until thickened; simmer about 5 minutes. Slowly stir in half-and-half. Add cheese, 1 cup at a time, mixing well after each addition, until cheese is melted.

Go ahead and try this out with some other kinds of cheeses, but don't use mozzarella as it will make the soup stringy and a real mess to eat. MCM

FRENCH BISTRO ONION SOUP

When it comes to onions, I'm pretty picky about how I like to eat them. My favorite way is when they're caramelized, because they're so much sweeter. That's why I love French onion soup. It starts off with plenty of caramelized onions that get added to a flavorful beef broth. Just before it's ready to serve, it's finished off with a slice of French bread and Swiss cheese. The results are bistro-worthy.

Serves 6

3 tablespoons butter

4 large onions, thinly sliced

6 cups beef broth

¼ teaspoon salt

½ teaspoon black pepper

½ cup grated Parmesan cheese

⅓ cup dry red wine

6 (1-inch) slices French bread, toasted

6 slices Swiss cheese

■ In a soup pot over medium heat, melt butter. Add onions and cook 20 to 25 minutes or until golden, stirring occasionally. (I know it seems like a long time, but it takes a while to get the onions golden.) Add broth, salt, and pepper; bring to a boil. Reduce heat to low, stir in Parmesan cheese and wine, and cook 3 to 5 minutes, or until cheese is melted and soup is heated through. (If you don't want to add the wine, you can use apple juice or cider instead.)

■ Preheat broiler. Place broiler-safe soup bowls, crocks, or ramekins on a baking sheet. Pour soup into crocks and top each with a slice of bread topped with Swiss cheese.

■ Broil 3 to 5 minutes, or until cheese is melted. Serve immediately.

COMFORTING BEEF BARLEY SOUP

Adding barley to soup is the perfect way to beef it up (pun intended!), since barley is just another grain that adds heartiness, in the same way that rice and noodles do. That's why, in the winter months, this is one of my favorite soups. Not only is it comforting, but one bowl is enough to leave you full and satisfied.

Serves 4 to 6

2 tablespoons vegetable oil

1 pound beef stew meat, cut into ½-inch chunks

1 onion, chopped

1 cup celery, sliced

3 carrots, diced

1 (14.5-ounce) can diced tomatoes, undrained

8 cups beef broth

½ teaspoon salt

½ teaspoon black pepper

¾ cup quick-cooking pearl barley

■ In a soup pot over high heat, heat oil until hot, but not smoking. Add beef, onion, celery, and carrots; sauté 6 to 8 minutes, or until they begin to brown. (Browning the meat and vegetables will make your soup more flavorful.)

■ Add the can of tomatoes (including the liquid), the beef broth, salt, and pepper; bring to a boil. Lower the heat to low and simmer 30 minutes, or until beef is so tender it falls apart, stirring occasionally.

■ Add barley and simmer an additional 15 to 20 minutes, or until barley is tender. Serve piping hot.

I've made this soup many times before a Sunday QVC appearance. I just put it together in the morning and reheat it when I get home from the show. MCM

HOMEMADE CHICKEN NOODLE SOUP

Everyone's got to know how to make a homemade chicken soup. I mean, what are you going to do if your neighbor gets sick and needs you to help nurse them back to health?! Exactly. Chicken soup is the answer to everything as far as I'm concerned; it can help cure a cold, soothe an upset stomach, or even put a smile on a sad friend's face. In fact, I'm thinking you should make extra of this, since it's so good and all.

Serves 6 to 8

1 (3- to 3-½-pound) chicken, cut into 8 pieces

12 cups cold water

3 carrots, cut into 1-inch chunks

2 celery stalks, cut into 1-inch chunks

1 onion, cut into 1-inch chunks

3 tablespoons chicken base (see note)

2 teaspoons salt

½ teaspoon black pepper

2 cups frozen home-style egg noodles

■ In a soup pot over high heat, combine all ingredients except noodles; bring to a boil. Reduce heat to low and simmer 1-½ hours, or until chicken falls off the bones easily.

■ Using tongs, remove chicken from soup; allow chicken to cool slightly. Remove the bones and skin, then cut or tear the chicken into bite-sized pieces, and return it to the soup.

■ Add noodles, right from the freezer, and heat 10-12 minutes, or until tender. (You can find these noodles in the freezer aisle right next to the other frozen pasta, like ravioli. If you can't find them, you can always add 2 cups of cooked wide egg noodles.)

Chicken base is just a form of highly concentrated chicken stock. In the grocery store, it's usually right next to the bouillon cubes. If you don't see it, don't be shy about asking someone where it is, or you can just use bouillon powder or cubes (just add according to your taste). MCM

LOADED BAKED POTATO SOUP

Crumbled bacon and shredded cheese could probably top anything without anyone complaining, but if I were to place a bet on what first came to mind when you thought of what they'd be good on, my money would be on "potato." Everyone knows that a loaded potato has to include bacon and cheese, and the same with loaded potato skins. So, why not follow suit with a loaded potato soup? It's thick, creamy, and delicious!

Serves 5 to 6

5 large baking potatoes

6 tablespoons butter

½ cup chopped onion

1 cup chopped celery

⅓ cup all-purpose flour

3 cups chicken broth

1 teaspoon salt

⅛ teaspoon black pepper

3 cups half-and-half

1 cup shredded cheddar cheese

4 bacon slices, cooked and crumbled

■ Preheat oven to 400 degrees F.

■ Prick each potato several times with a fork and place on baking sheet. Bake for 55 to 60 minutes, or until fork tender. (My toaster oven works great for this.) Let cool slightly, then cut into ½-inch cubes.

■ Meanwhile, in a soup pot over medium heat, melt butter and sauté onion and celery until soft. Stir in flour and cook for 1 minute. Add chicken broth, salt, and pepper, and cook until thickened. Slowly stir in half-and-half and add potatoes.

■ Simmer over low heat until heated through and thickened. When ready to serve, top with cheese and bacon. (You can even add a dollop of sour cream if that's your thing!)

The next time your oven is on, go ahead and bake a few extra potatoes. That way, your potatoes will be ready for cubing, and you'll have saved all that baking time. MCM

SLOW COOKER ITALIAN WEDDING SOUP

For the record, I have never been served this soup at an Italian wedding. The reason why it's named that way has to do with the happy "marriage" of the ingredients it's made from. Basically, the greens go well with the meat. Who would've thought? Anyway, I don't see why more people aren't putting this on their reception menu. A bowl in front of every guest would really help boost the love in the room.

Serves 8 to 10

6 (10-½-ounce) cans condensed chicken broth

4 cups water

1 (14-ounce) package cocktail-sized frozen meatballs

2 eggs, beaten

4 cups freshly chopped escarole or spinach

¾ cup grated Parmesan cheese, plus extra for garnish (optional)

■ In a 4-½-quart or larger slow cooker, combine broth, water, and meatballs. Cover and cook on HIGH 2-½ hours or on LOW 6 hours, or until meatballs are heated through.

■ Remove cover and slowly stir in egg, forming thin strands. Stir in escarole and ¾ cup Parmesan cheese. Serve immediately; top with additional Parmesan cheese, if desired.

BEEFY BEAN CHILI

Whether it's right or wrong to put beans in chili isn't for me to decide. All I know is that the beans really help make this dish, so call it what you want, but give it a try first. I know that once you do, you'll be hooked. You see the ladle in the photo? I wouldn't be surprised if that's what you used in lieu of a spoon.

Serves 4 to 5

1 pound lean ground beef

1 onion, chopped

2 (15-ounce) cans kidney beans, undrained

1 (28-ounce) can diced tomatoes, undrained

1 (15-ounce) can tomato sauce

1 (4-ounce) can chopped green chilies, undrained

2 tablespoons chili powder

1 teaspoon ground cumin

½ teaspoon salt

½ teaspoon black pepper

■ In a soup pot over medium-high heat, brown ground beef and onion 5 to 7 minutes. Make sure you break it up as it cooks, so you end up with crumbles.

■ Add remaining ingredients, reduce heat to medium-low, and cook 50 to 60 minutes, or until chili is thickened, stirring occasionally. (This is one of those dishes that seems to taste better the more you cook it, so please don't rush perfection.)

This would be a great recipe to make for a friendly neighborhood cook-off, especially since the recipe can be doubled or tripled really easily. Don't forget to set out some different toppings, such as shredded cheese, sour cream, corn chips, jalapeño peppers, and a variety of hot sauces. MCM

BLONDE CHICKEN CHILI

Blonde chili is like a lighter version of traditional red chili. I've tried to convince myself into thinking it's "diet chili," but, if I'm being honest, it's really just another excuse for me to have chili more often. This one is made with plenty of chicken, white beans, tomatoes, and some flavorful spices. It's even got a spicy kick to it.

Serves 5 to 6

1 tablespoon vegetable oil

1-½ pounds boneless, skinless chicken breasts, cut into ½-inch cubes

1 onion, chopped

3 cloves garlic, minced

½ teaspoon salt

¼ teaspoon black pepper

4 (16-ounce) cans Great Northern beans, undrained

1 (14.5-ounce) can diced tomatoes, undrained

2 cups chicken broth

1 tablespoon hot sauce

2 teaspoons ground cumin

2 teaspoons chili powder

1 teaspoon dried oregano

■ In a soup pot over high heat, heat oil until hot. Add chicken, onion, garlic, salt and pepper; sauté 5 to 6 minutes, or until chicken is no longer pink. Add remaining ingredients and bring to a boil.

■ Reduce heat to low and simmer 45 to 50 minutes, or until chili thickens slightly, stirring occasionally.

I like topping this with a dollop of sour cream to make it extra-creamy delicious.

SUMMER'S SHRIMP GAZPACHO

There are a couple of reasons why this soup is a summer must-have. First, it's made with produce that is at its peak in the summer, which means you'll either have everything you need growing in your garden or you'll find it at a good price in the supermarket. Plus, since it's chilled, it serves as a tasty way to beat the heat.

Serves 8 to 10

1 (46-ounce) can vegetable juice

1 (14.5-ounce) can diced tomatoes, drained

1 large cucumber, peeled, seeded, and diced

1 green bell pepper, diced

5 scallions, thinly sliced

3 cloves garlic, minced

⅓ cup white vinegar

1 tablespoon olive oil

2 teaspoons Worcestershire sauce

1 tablespoon chopped fresh dill

½ teaspoon hot pepper sauce

1 (10-ounce) package frozen cooked salad shrimp, thawed

■ In a large bowl, combine all ingredients; mix well.

■ Cover and chill at least 4 hours before serving.

Gazpacho can be made ahead of time and placed in the fridge for a few days. That's great since it means I can have it ready for whenever I'm craving something flavorful and refreshing. MCM

RESTAURANT-FAMOUS CAESAR SALAD

Is there a restaurant somewhere in the world that doesn't have this salad on the menu? And if there is, why not?! This is a classic! The key to a great Caesar salad is all in the dressing, since otherwise it's pretty basic. I like to make my own creamy version of the dressing, and sometimes, even my own croutons. It makes a world of difference.

Serves 4 to 5

1 cup mayonnaise

½ cup milk

2 tablespoons fresh lemon juice

½ cup plus 1 tablespoon shredded Parmesan cheese, divided

2 cloves garlic, minced

½ teaspoon salt

½ teaspoon black pepper

1 head romaine lettuce, cut into bite-sized pieces

2 cups croutons

1 (2-ounce) can anchovies in oil, drained (optional)

■ In a medium bowl, combine mayonnaise, milk, lemon juice, ½ cup Parmesan cheese, the garlic, salt, and pepper. Whisk until smooth and creamy; set aside. (Starting with the mayo makes this nice and creamy without having to dig out the food processor.)

■ Place romaine in a large bowl and add some of the dressing; gently toss to coat well. If desired, add more dressing or refrigerate leftover dressing for a later use. It can be refrigerated for about a week.

■ Top with croutons, remaining Parmesan cheese and anchovies, if desired. Serve immediately.

To make your own croutons, just place 4 cups of stale bread chunks (about 8 slices any type of bread) in a bowl. In a small bowl, combine ½ stick melted butter (or you can use ¼ cup olive oil), 1 teaspoon garlic powder, ¼ teaspoon Italian seasoning, ½ teaspoon salt, and ¼ teaspoon black pepper. Toss the bread with the butter mixture and place on a baking sheet in a preheated 375-degree oven. Bake 15 to 20 minutes, or until they're crunchy and golden. Let cool, top your salad, or store in an airtight container. MCM

TASTE OF TUSCANY BREAD SALAD

One of the best parts about visiting Italy every summer with my family is eating all of the good food the country has to offer. Most people think of pizza and pasta when they think of traditional Italian food, but there's so much more! This salad comes from the Tuscany region and is made with lots of garden-fresh ingredients that are tossed together with bread cubes before soaking in an Italian vinaigrette. It makes for a light and tasty start to any meal.

Serves 4 to 6

¼ cup olive oil

½ teaspoon garlic powder

8 (1-inch-thick) slices Italian bread, cut into 1-inch cubes

6 plum tomatoes, chopped

1 cucumber, seeded and cubed

½ red onion, thinly sliced

¼ cup chopped fresh basil

¾ cup Italian dressing

■ Preheat oven to 375 degrees F.

■ In a large bowl, combine olive oil and garlic powder. Add bread cubes and toss to coat. (Any bread works, so don't feel like it has to be Italian. I've made it with everything from sourdough to herb breads.) Place on baking sheet and bake 15 to 20 minutes, or until bread is crispy and golden brown, turning once during baking.

■ In a large bowl, combine crispy bread cubes and remaining ingredients; toss gently. Let stand 20 minutes before serving, so the dressing can seep into the toasted bread.

If you've got the time and would like to make a homemade Italian dressing, here's my recipe: All you do is whisk together ½ cup olive oil, ¼ cup red wine vinegar, ½ teaspoon garlic powder, ½ teaspoon onion powder, ½ teaspoon salt, ¼ teaspoon pepper, and 1 teaspoon lemon juice. You can also put all of the ingredients into a dressing shaker bottle and just shake them up! MCM

THREE BERRIES SPINACH SALAD

This is one sweet summer salad! It's loaded with three different types of berries, each of which add their own distinctive flavors and sweetness to the mix. Plus, there's candied pecans, creamy goat cheese crumbles, and a simple balsamic-sugar glaze that brings it all together. I can't make any guarantees, but if you make this, you might just have a "berry" good summer.

Serves 4 to 5

2 cups balsamic vinegar

1 cup light brown sugar

1 (10-ounce) package baby spinach

½ cup strawberries, sliced

½ cup raspberries

½ cup blueberries

½ cup candied pecans

4 ounces goat cheese, crumbled

■ In a medium saucepan over high heat, bring balsamic vinegar to a boil. Stir in brown sugar, reduce heat to low, and simmer 12 to 15 minutes, or until liquid is reduced and slightly thickened. Remove from heat and let cool.

■ On a serving platter or on individual plates, top spinach with berries, pecans, and goat cheese. Drizzle with some of the balsamic glaze and serve. (A little goes a long way, so use it sparingly.)

There will be a good amount of the glaze leftover, so make sure you store the extra in the fridge. And besides putting it on the salad, it's also amazing on grilled chicken, fish, steamed veggies, or even drizzled on crusty bread. MCM

TOSSED TACO BOWL

One way to do taco night is to make a build-your-own-tacos buffet or serve my Red Chile Enchiladas (page 102). Another way is to make this simple Tossed Taco Bowl, which is pretty much everything that's great about tacos in one easy-to-throw-together salad. It's great for potluck dinners and family picnics because it feeds a lot of people without involving a whole lot of work.

Serves 6 to 8

1 pound ground beef

1 (1-ounce) package dry taco seasoning mix

1 head iceberg lettuce, chopped (about 8 cups)

2 cups (8 ounces) shredded Mexican cheese blend

1 (15.5-ounce) can kidney beans, rinsed and drained

2 large tomatoes, diced (about 2 cups)

2 (2.25-ounce) cans sliced black olives, drained

1 (16-ounce) bottle sweet-and-spicy French salad dressing

2 cups coarsely crushed tortilla chips

■ In a medium skillet over medium high heat, brown ground beef with taco seasoning, cooking until meat is crumbled and no pink remains; drain and cool.

■ When the meat is cool, in a large salad bowl, toss together all ingredients except dressing and tortilla chips. Right before serving, drizzle on the dressing and toss to coat well. Top each serving with crushed tortilla chips and enjoy.

CRISP 'N' CREAMY CUCUMBER SALAD

I start making cucumber salads the minute the weather starts to get warm. They're just so light-tasting and refreshing. This is a great basic recipe if you've never made one before. It's a little sweet, a little tangy, and a whole lot crisp 'n' creamy. I sometimes lighten this up even more by substituting sour cream for Greek yogurt and using stevia in place of sugar. Either way, it's very tasty.

Serves 6 to 8

2 cucumbers, thinly sliced (see note)

4 scallions, thinly sliced

½ small red bell pepper, chopped

¼ cup sour cream

3 tablespoons white vinegar

3 tablespoons sugar

1-¼ teaspoons salt

¼ teaspoon black pepper

■ In a medium bowl, combine cucumbers, scallions, and red pepper.

■ To make dressing, in a small bowl, combine remaining ingredients. Toss the dressing with the cucumber mixture; cover and chill at least 2 hours. Before serving, toss again to keep the dressing nice and creamy.

It's really up to you whether you peel the cucumbers or not. I like to leave the skin on since it's full of fiber-rich nutrients. Plus, it adds a nice color contrast to the creamy dressing. MCM

REFRIGERATOR ANTIPASTO SALAD

The most important thing to remember about this salad is that there's no right or wrong way to go about it. You can mix and match with just about anything you've got in the fridge, although the combination below is one of my favorites (it's no coincidence that they're all traditional Italian ingredients!). Since this salad is also super-quick to throw together, it's great for last-minute company.

Serves 6 to 8

10 cups mixed greens, cut-up

2 tomatoes, cut into chunks

6 (1-ounce) slices provolone cheese, cut into strips

¼ pound Genoa salami, cut into strips

1 (14-ounce) can artichoke hearts, drained and quartered

½ cup roasted red peppers, drained and cut into strips

1 (5.75-ounce) can large pitted black olives, drained

½ cup pepperoncini, drained

¾ cup Italian dressing

■ In a large bowl, place all ingredients except dressing; toss gently until well combined.

■ Pour desired amount of dressing over salad; toss gently until evenly coated. Serve immediately.

If you would like to make a homemade vinaigrette, see page 68 (Taste of Tuscany Bread Salad). MCM

SOUTHWESTERN QUINOA SALAD

Here's how you become a quinoa convert: First, you make this salad. Second, you put it in your mouth. That's it. I should have known that pairing quinoa with some of my favorite Southwestern flavors would make me a fan. Now, I love making this salad for almost any occasion. It's simple, vibrant, and flavorful. (Plus, the zesty dressing is to-die-for!)

Serves 5 to 6

2 cups water

1 cup quinoa

⅓ cup olive oil

2 tablespoons lime juice

2 teaspoons ground cumin

¾ teaspoon salt

¼ teaspoon black pepper

1 (15-ounce) can black beans, drained and rinsed

1-½ cups cherry tomatoes, cut in half

4 scallions, thinly sliced

1 avocado, cut into chunks

2 tablespoons chopped fresh cilantro

■ In a medium saucepan over high heat, bring water and quinoa to a boil. Reduce heat to low, cover, and simmer 15 to 20 minutes, or until all water is absorbed. Let cool.

■ To make dressing, in a small bowl, whisk oil, lime juice, cumin, salt, and pepper; set aside.

■ In a large bowl, combine quinoa and remaining ingredients. Pour dressing over mixture and toss until evenly coated. Refrigerate until chilled.

CRUNCHY BROCCOLI SALAD

I love crunchy textures, and I'm always trying to think of new ways to incorporate them into my meals. In this salad I went all crunchy. I use naturally crunchy ingredients like fresh broccoli, radishes, and nuts and toss them with one unexpected crunchy ingredient...ramen noodles. Your bites may be a little noisy, but it's so delicious you won't even care!

Serves 6 to 7

1 (3-ounce) package ramen noodle soup mix

½ stick butter

1 cup walnuts or pecans, chopped

3 cups fresh broccoli florets

½ head romaine lettuce, cut into 1-inch pieces

2 radishes, thinly sliced

4 scallions, sliced

1 (8-ounce) bottle raspberry vinaigrette dressing

■ Break ramen noodles into pieces in unopened package. Carefully open package and remove seasoning packet; reserve for another use.

■ In a large skillet over medium-high heat, melt butter; add ramen noodles and walnuts, and sauté until lightly browned. Drain on paper towels.

■ In a large bowl, toss together noodle mixture, broccoli, lettuce, radishes, and scallions. Add ¼ cup dressing; toss to coat. Serve with remaining dressing, as desired. (If fresh raspberries are in season, go ahead and top each serving with a few to add a little extra tartness.)

This salad always gets someone to say, "I didn't know you could eat ramen noodles that way!" Well, you can! Ramen is precooked before it's packaged, which means you can eat it however you want. MCM

There's plenty of "fowl" language in this chapter (sorry, I couldn't resist!). If you're thinking of serving chicken for dinner, then I've got some ideas that will keep them from squawking (okay, okay, I'm done now!). MCM

CHICKEN & TURKEY

ITALIAN-STYLE CHICKEN ONE POT

Forget about making a bunch of different side dishes to go along with this recipe, because it's really hearty all on its own. Aside from the juicy dark meat chicken, it's loaded up with plenty of potatoes, onion, tomatoes, and an Italian-favorite, cannellini beans. And since everything gets cooked together in one pot, you know every bite is going to be packed with flavor.

Serves 4 to 5

2 tablespoons olive oil

½ teaspoon salt

¼ teaspoon black pepper

3-½ pounds chicken thighs and drumsticks (about 8 pieces)

1 onion, chopped

1 (14-ounce) can cannellini beans, drained

4 potatoes, peeled and cut into 1-inch chunks

1 (28-ounce) can diced tomatoes, undrained

2 tablespoons tomato paste

2 teaspoons dried tarragon (see note)

2 teaspoons garlic powder

¼ teaspoon crushed red pepper

■ In a large pot or Dutch oven over medium-high heat, heat oil. Sprinkle salt and pepper over chicken and sauté 10 minutes, or until browned on each side, turning halfway through cooking.

■ Add onion, give everything a good stir, and sauté about 2 minutes. Add remaining ingredients to chicken; mix well.

■ Bring to a boil, then reduce heat to low and simmer, uncovered, 25 to 30 minutes, or until chicken is tender and cooked through.

Dried herbs are easy and convenient, but when I have fresh herbs on hand, I do prefer to make the swap! A good rule of thumb is, if a recipe calls for one teaspoon of dried herbs, you would use one tablespoon of fresh in its place. MCM

ROSEMARY-STUFFED ROASTED CHICKEN

You know what makes a great roasted chicken? Crispy skin, juicy meat, and lots of flavor throughout. If any of these is missing, then you're just going to be let down at some point throughout dinner. The good news is, I've got all of my bases covered in this recipe. I've even gone a little above and beyond by adding some white wine—it gives it a fancy touch.

Serves 4 to 5

2 tablespoons vegetable oil

1 teaspoon paprika

½ teaspoon garlic powder

½ teaspoon onion powder

½ teaspoon salt

½ teaspoon black pepper

1 (4- to 4-½-pound) chicken

4 sprigs fresh rosemary, plus extra for garnish

2 lemons, cut in half, plus slices for garnish

½ cup white wine

- Preheat oven to 350 degrees F. In a small bowl, combine oil, paprika, garlic powder, onion powder, salt, and pepper; mix well.

- Place chicken in a roasting pan and rub with seasoning mixture. (Yes, you can use your hands!) Stuff 4 rosemary sprigs and 2 lemon halves inside the chicken's cavity. Squeeze remaining lemon halves over the chicken, then place in pan. Pour wine over chicken.

- Roast, uncovered, 1-½ hours, or until the skin is crispy and juices run clear, basting occasionally with pan juices (I just do this with a soup spoon). Remove from oven and discard rosemary and lemon halves.

- Place chicken on platter, garnish with the extra rosemary sprigs and sliced lemon. Allow to rest 5 minutes before cutting into pieces. Serve with pan drippings.

THE CRISPIEST FRIED CHICKEN

When I take a bite out of fried chicken, I want to hear it crunch. I want it to be so crispy that people around me wonder whether I'm really eating fried chicken or I've just snuck some crunchy potato chips into my mouth. If your fried chicken doesn't do this for you, then it's time to retire that recipe and give mine a try.

Serves 4 to 5

1 (3- to 3-½-pound) chicken, cut into 8 pieces

½ cup milk

1 egg

1 cup all-purpose flour

1 tablespoon salt

1 teaspoon black pepper

1 teaspoon poultry seasoning

3 cups vegetable oil

■ In a large bowl, soak chicken in ice cold water for 30 minutes. Drain well and pat dry with paper towels.

■ In a large bowl, combine milk and egg; mix well. Add chicken, coating completely. In another large bowl, combine flour, salt, pepper, and poultry seasoning; mix well. Remove chicken from milk mixture one piece at a time, shaking off the excess, then toss in flour mixture, coating completely.

■ Meanwhile, in a large deep skillet over medium heat, heat oil until hot, but not smoking. (Be sure oil does not fill skillet more than half way.) If you have a thermometer, I recommend the oil to be 350 degrees F.

■ Carefully place chicken in oil and cook 20 to 22 minutes, or until coating is golden and chicken is no longer pink. Drain on a wire rack over a baking sheet. Serve immediately or warm in a low oven until heated through.

A Southern friend of mine once told me that the trick to crispy fried chicken is to make sure it's soaked in really cold water before breading it (don't forget to drain it really well!). Also, make sure the oil is plenty hot without smoking. MCM

HOMESTYLE CHICKEN POT PIE

I don't know anybody who looks at chicken pot pie and doesn't smile. The way I see it, chicken pot pie is a beautiful little package of happiness. I mean, it's a pie...with dinner inside! You just can't get any better than that. Whenever I'm craving a taste of home or need a little extra comfort, I always turn to this—it's really one of my all-time faves.

Serves 4 to 6

1 (14.1-ounce) package refrigerated pie crusts

2 pounds boneless, skinless chicken breasts, cut into 1-inch chunks

1 cup frozen sliced carrots

1 cup frozen green peas

1 stick butter

⅓ cup chopped onion

⅓ cup all-purpose flour

½ teaspoon celery seed

¾ teaspoon salt

¼ teaspoon black pepper

1-¾ cups chicken broth

¾ cup milk

■ Preheat oven to 425 degrees F.

■ Place chicken in a large saucepan with enough water to cover. Over high heat, boil for 10 minutes. Stir in carrots and peas and continue boiling for 2 minutes. Drain in a colander and set aside. Don't worry about thawing the veggies first, since you don't need to!

■ In the same saucepan over medium heat, melt butter and cook onions for 5 minutes, or until tender. Add flour, celery seed, salt, and pepper, and whisk for 1 minute, or until golden. Slowly stir in chicken broth and milk and cook until thickened, stirring constantly. Remove from heat, and stir in chicken mixture. Place 1 pie crust in a 9-inch deep dish pie plate. Pour chicken filling into pie crust.

■ Place second pie crust on top of mixture; seal and flute edges. With a knife, cut 4 (1-inch) slits in top of crust. This will allow the steam to escape while cooking and prevent the top crust from getting soggy. Bake 30 to 35 minutes, or until crust is golden brown and filling is bubbly. Let sit 5 minutes before serving.

CREAMY CHICKEN AND RICE CASSEROLE

I suggest you start looking for a good spot to settle into before you get to baking this casserole, because once it comes out, and you've sat down with your plate, you're going to have a hard time wanting to get back up. This is just one of those feel-good casseroles that everyone should have a recipe for. It's soul-satisfying all the way to the very last bite.

Serves 4 to 5

1 (10-¾-ounce) can cream of mushroom soup

1 (10-¾-ounce) can cream of celery soup

1 cup uncooked long-grain rice

1 envelope onion soup mix (from a 2-ounce box)

1-¼ cups water

1 clove garlic, crushed

1 teaspoon chopped fresh parsley

1 teaspoon Worcestershire sauce

1 (3-½- to 4-pound) chicken, cut into 8 pieces

Paprika for sprinkling

■ Preheat oven to 350 degrees F. Coat a 9- x 13-inch baking dish with cooking spray.

■ In a large bowl, mix together soups, rice, soup mix, water, garlic, parsley, and Worcestershire sauce.

■ Pour mixture into baking dish. Place chicken on top of the soup mixture. (Yes, I'm sure the chicken goes on top.) Sprinkle with paprika, then cover tightly with aluminum foil.

■ Bake 1-¼ hours. (No need to check on it during this time.) Uncover carefully, as steam will be very hot. You'll know it's done when it's bubbling hot and the chicken is no longer pink. Serve chicken with flavor-packed rice mixture.

Sometimes I add a cup of thinly sliced fresh carrots or celery (or both) to the sauce before baking this, to help make sure I get in my five-a-day when it comes to veggies. MCM

KENTUCKY BBQ ROASTED CHICKEN

The weather doesn't always make it easy for me to go outside and fire up the grill, but that's never stopped me from eating barbecue whenever I want! On those days, I just make this oven-roasted chicken covered in a homemade, Kentucky-inspired, BBQ sauce. The sauce is just the right amount of tangy and sweet, and has a uniquely delicious flavor thanks to the bourbon and Worcestershire sauce. It's good enough to want to lick your fingers clean!

Serves 4 to 5

1 (3-½ to 4-pound) chicken, cut into 8 pieces, with skin removed

1 tablespoon all-purpose flour

1 onion, finely chopped

½ cup Dijon mustard

½ cup packed brown sugar

¼ cup bourbon

2 teaspoons Worcestershire sauce

½ teaspoon salt

- Preheat oven to 400 degrees F. Coat a 9- x 13-inch baking dish with cooking spray.

- Place chicken in baking dish and sprinkle evenly with flour.

- In a small bowl, mix together the remaining ingredients. Pour evenly over chicken, making sure you cover all of the pieces evenly. Cover tightly with aluminum foil.

- Roast 30 minutes, then uncover and continue cooking 30 to 35 minutes, or until juices run clear in the chicken.

Feel free to use all dark meat or all white meat if you prefer one over the other. MCM

GREEK SALAD CHICKEN PITAS

The secret to making the best chicken pitas you've ever tasted is all in what you use to marinate the chicken, and the marinade in this recipe is phenomenal. The juicy and flavorful chicken tenders are the perfect complement to the Greek salad ingredients, and to tie it all together I use plenty of tzatziki sauce. This is a fantastic, fresh and healthy lunch option.

Serves 4

¼ cup olive oil

1 teaspoon lemon juice

4 cloves garlic, minced

1 teaspoon dried oregano

¼ teaspoon salt

¼ teaspoon black pepper

1-½ pounds chicken tenders

4 pita breads

2 cups chopped romaine lettuce

1 cup diced tomato

¼ cup sliced black olives, drained

2 tablespoons chopped red onion

1 cup tzatziki sauce (see note)

■ In a resealable plastic bag, combine oil, lemon juice, garlic, oregano, salt, and pepper; mix well. Add chicken and toss until evenly coated. Refrigerate at least 1 hour.

■ In a large skillet over medium-high heat, cook chicken for 6 to 8 minutes, or until no longer pink in center, turning occasionally.

■ Meanwhile, wrap the pita in foil and warm in a 300-degree oven for about 10 minutes.

■ Fill each pita evenly with lettuce, tomato, chicken, olives, and onion. Top with tzatziki sauce and serve.

Tzatziki is a Greek, yogurt-based sauce made with cucumbers, fresh herbs, and other ingredients. While you can find it already prepared in your supermarket, it's so easy to make, I usually make my own. All you need to do is mix together 1 cup of plain Greek yogurt, 2 teaspoons of lemon juice, 1 cup of chopped or grated cucumber, 2 cloves of minced garlic, 1 teaspoon of chopped fresh mint, and a pinch of salt. MCM

AWESOME CHICKEN AND VEGGIES

I know the struggles of trying to get your family to eat their veggies. Luckily, I've found that this recipe can make anyone love their veggies (no bribing necessary). The combination of chicken, sausage, and a medley of fresh vegetables makes for a perfectly delicious meal. In the words of one of my happy taste testers, "This is awesome!"

Serves 4 to 6

1 pound Italian sausage, cut into ½-inch pieces

2 bell peppers, cut into chunks

1-½ pounds boneless, skinless chicken breasts, cut into 1-inch chunks

1 onion, cut into thick slices

4 cloves garlic, coarsely chopped

½ teaspoon salt

½ teaspoon black pepper

2 tomatoes, cut into 2-inch chunks

¼ pound sliced mushrooms

2 tablespoons fresh chopped parsley

■ In a Dutch oven or soup pot over medium-high heat, cook sausage and bell peppers 10 minutes, or until browned, stirring occasionally.

■ Add the chicken, onion, garlic, salt, and black pepper. Cook 8 to 10 minutes, or until chicken is no longer pink, stirring occasionally.

■ Stir in the tomatoes, mushrooms, and parsley. Reduce heat to low, cover, and simmer 5 to 7 minutes, or until heated through.

This is one of those dishes that I like to change up a little every time to keep things exciting. First of all, I like to mix up the color of peppers based on which are on sale. And when it comes to the sausage, I vary how hot the sausage is based on who I'm serving it to. My kids like it mild, but my friends always prefer a spicier kind. MCM

WEEKNIGHT CHICKEN MILANESE

Chicken Milanese is one of those chicken dinners you find on every Italian restaurant menu and assume is a fancy dish (Mila-who?). But really, it's just a breaded chicken cutlet that's fried until it's golden and delicious. It makes for a great weeknight meal, especially since it's served best with a simple salad of mixed greens and tomatoes.

Serves 4

2 boneless, skinless chicken breasts

¼ teaspoon salt, divided

¼ teaspoon black pepper, divided

¼ cup whole milk

2 eggs

1 cup seasoned panko bread crumbs

½ cup all-purpose flour

2 tablespoons butter

2 tablespoons olive oil

Mixed greens for serving

½ cup cherry tomatoes, cut in half

Balsamic vinegar for drizzling

½ cup shaved or grated Parmesan cheese

½ lemon

■ Place the chicken breasts on a cutting board and, with a sharp knife, carefully cut each chicken breast in half horizontally, so that you end up with four cutlets. Since we want these really thin, place each cutlet between 2 sheets of wax paper and use the smooth side of a meat mallet to pound them until they're very thin.

■ In a shallow dish, combine 1/8 teaspoon each of salt and pepper. In another shallow dish, whisk together milk and eggs. Place bread crumbs in a third shallow dish.

■ Sprinkle both sides of cutlets with remaining salt and pepper. Generously coat them with flour, then dip into the egg mixture, followed by the bread crumbs. Make sure you firmly pat on the bread crumbs, so that they stick. Lay the coated cutlets on a baking sheet until ready to cook.

■ In a large skillet over medium heat, heat 1 tablespoon butter and 1 tablespoon oil until melted and hot. Add 2 cutlets and cook 2 to 3 minutes per side, or until breading is golden brown and chicken is cooked through; remove to a platter. Add remaining butter and oil, and cook remaining cutlets.

■ When ready to serve, place chicken on plates, top with mixed greens and tomatoes, drizzle with balsamic vinegar, and finish with Parmesan cheese and a squeeze of lemon.

CRISPY & CRUNCHY CHICKEN CASSEROLE

How often do you cook with water chestnuts? Sure, you've probably had them in some Asian dishes, but if you've never used them in any other way you're really missing out! Well, I'm about to change that. This dish gets its crispy-crunchiness from the water chestnuts and slivered almonds that are mixed in, as well as the French-fried onions sprinkled on top. It's a perfect contrast to the casserole's creaminess, and makes for a mouthwatering change of pace.

Serves 5 to 6

3 cups chopped cooked chicken

2 cups chopped celery

1 cup (4 ounces) shredded cheddar cheese

1 cup sour cream

1 cup mayonnaise

1 (4-ounce) can water chestnuts, drained and chopped

1 (10-¾-ounce) can cream of chicken soup

½ cup slivered almonds

1 (6-ounce) package French-fried onions

▉ Preheat oven to 350 degrees F. Coat a 9- x 13-inch baking dish with cooking spray.

▉ In a large bowl, combine chicken, celery, cheese, sour cream, mayonnaise, water chestnuts, soup, and almonds. Spoon into baking dish.

▉ Bake, uncovered, 30 minutes. Top evenly with French-fried onions and bake 5 more minutes to allow the onions to get extra crispy. Let stand 5 minutes before serving.

LONG ISLAND CHICKEN CUTLET SANDWICHES

This is MY sandwich. Sometimes I call it my "Long Island Classic," since I order it every time I'm in the area to visit family. I don't even think about another sandwich when I'm at the deli. But, if you ever do see me there and it looks like I might be ordering something new (the atrocity!), feel free to remind me about "the lunch that never lets you down." I'll know exactly what you're talking about.

Serves 4

¾ cup bread crumbs

½ cup grated Parmesan cheese

2 tablespoons chopped fresh parsley

½ teaspoon garlic powder

2 eggs

4 boneless, skinless chicken breasts, flattened to ½-inch thickness

Cooking spray

4 leaves romaine lettuce

2 tomatoes, sliced

4 slices Swiss cheese

½ cup Thousand Island dressing

4 sub rolls, cut in half

▪ Preheat oven to 375 degrees F. Coat a baking sheet with cooking spray.

▪ In a shallow dish, combine bread crumbs, Parmesan cheese, parsley, and garlic powder; mix thoroughly. In another shallow dish, beat eggs. Coat cutlets in egg, then in bread crumb mixture, patting gently so they really stick on.

▪ Place cutlets on baking sheet. Lightly spray chicken with cooking spray and bake 20 to 25 minutes, or until golden and no pink remains.

▪ Evenly place lettuce, tomato, chicken, Swiss cheese, and dressing on each roll; serve immediately.

If you find yourself out of Thousand Island dressing, just mix 1 cup of mayonnaise, ¼ cup of sweet relish, and ¼ cup of ketchup. Crisis averted! MCM

BBQ CHIP-CRUSTED CHICKEN FINGERS

Believe it or not, I didn't have my first chicken fingers until I was in college (I know, right?). Once I did, I was hooked. The first time I had them they were the traditional kind, breaded with breadcrumbs, but after some experimentation, I decided to try using potato chips instead (not just regular potato chips, the BBQ kind!). They give the chicken a perfectly crispy crust that's really delicious and a little zesty.

Serves 4 to 6

1 (7-¾-ounce) bag BBQ-flavored potato chips, finely crushed

½ teaspoon onion powder

½ teaspoon salt

¼ teaspoon black pepper

2 eggs

1-½ pounds chicken tenders

Cooking spray

■ Preheat oven to 400 degrees F. Coat a baking sheet with cooking spray.

■ In a shallow dish, combine chips, onion powder, salt, and pepper; mix well. In another shallow dish, beat eggs. Dip the chicken into the egg, then roll in potato chip mixture, coating evenly on all sides. Place on baking sheet. Lightly spray chicken with cooking spray. Spraying the chicken allows it to "oven fry."

■ Bake 15 to 18 minutes, or until crispy and chicken is no longer pink in center. Serve as-is or with your favorite dipping sauce.

My dip of choice for these chicken fingers is a homemade pineapple dipping sauce. It's easy to throw together! All you have to do is mix together ¼ cup of pineapple preserves, ¼ cup of sour cream, ¼ cup of mayonnaise, and ⅛ teaspoon of salt in a small bowl. Put it in the fridge to chill while the chicken is baking and serve when you're ready to eat.   MCM

RESTAURANT-WORTHY STUFFED CHICKEN

This is for all of you who've left a restaurant wondering, "Why can't I make something like this at home?" You can! I wanted to share this Mediterranean-style chicken recipe with you, so you can see how easy it is to whip up something this fresh-tasting and fancy-looking in your own kitchen. Every bite is packed with the rich flavors of fresh herbs, goat cheese, sun-dried tomatoes, and more. Your dinner guests are definitely going to be impressed.

Serves 4

10 butter-flavored crackers

1 teaspoon butter, melted

¼ cup sun-dried tomatoes in oil, drained and chopped

½ cup olive oil

2 tablespoons chopped fresh parsley

2 cloves garlic, peeled

¼ teaspoon salt, plus extra for sprinkling

¼ teaspoon black pepper, plus extra for sprinkling

4 boneless, skinless chicken breasts, butterflied (see note)

1 (4-ounce) package goat cheese, sliced into 4 pieces

4 basil leaves

■ Preheat oven to 350 degrees F. Coat a 9- x 13-inch baking dish with cooking spray. In a resealable plastic bag, crush crackers; add butter, mix, and set aside.

■ In a blender or food processor, combine sun-dried tomatoes, oil, parsley, garlic, salt, and pepper; process until everything is finely chopped.

■ Place chicken breasts on a cutting board. Open them up like a book then lightly sprinkle both sides with additional salt and pepper. Place 1 piece of goat cheese on 1 half of each chicken breast and top each with a basil leaf. Evenly spoon 1 tablespoon of the sun-dried tomato mixture over each basil leaf. Fold 1 side of the chicken breast over the filling and carefully place stuffed breasts in baking dish. Spoon remaining sun-dried tomato mixture evenly over chicken and sprinkle with cracker topping.

■ Bake 25 to 30 minutes, or until chicken is cooked through and no pink remains.

To butterfly a chicken breast, lay the breast on a cutting board and place one hand on top to keep it secured. Then, using a sharp knife, carefully cut the breast horizontally, about ¾ of the way through, so that it opens like a book. Repeat with each chicken breast. MCM

RED CHILE ENCHILADAS

I hate to break it to you Philadelphia, but we've got to work on getting some better take-out options. I had such a hard time finding great Mexican take-out one night that I decided I was just going to make it myself. Now, on those nights when I'd rather stay in, I make these easy red enchiladas stuffed with rice, beans, and some ground turkey. You'll be doing the happy dance before this one is even out of the oven.

Serves 8

1 (19-ounce) can red enchilada sauce

1 (10-½-ounce) can cream of chicken soup

1 (10-½-ounce) can cream of mushroom soup

1 tablespoon olive oil

1 pound ground turkey

1 (8.5-ounce) package pre-cooked Spanish rice, heated according to package directions (see note)

1 (16-ounce) can refried beans

8 (6-inch) flour tortillas

1 cup shredded Colby-Jack cheese

■ Preheat oven to 350 degrees F. Coat a 9- x 13-inch baking dish with cooking spray. In a large bowl, combine enchilada sauce and soups; mix well. Evenly spread 1 cup sauce mixture in baking dish; set aside.

■ In a large skillet over medium heat, heat oil and cook turkey for 6 to 8 minutes, or until no longer pink, stirring occasionally so the turkey crumbles. Stir in rice and beans.

■ Spoon an equal amount of mixture down the center of each tortilla and roll up, placing seam side down in baking dish. Pour remaining sauce over tortillas. Cover with aluminum foil and bake 35 minutes. Remove from oven, sprinkle with cheese, and bake an additional 5 to 10 minutes, or until cheese is melted.

Check the grains and rice aisle of your supermarket for pre-cooked Spanish rice. It's available in pouches and is really convenient in recipes like this. However, if you want to make your own homemade Spanish rice or start with a mix, you'll need to end up with about 4 cups. MCM

5-NAPKIN HONEY-GLAZED CHICKEN

If you eat these with your hands, prepare to get sticky! I'm really generous when it comes to coating my drumsticks with the honey-garlic glaze. Sometimes, I even make a double batch, so I have extra to drizzle on during dinner. The only problem is, I've got to make sure to keep plenty of napkins nearby, since one definitely won't cut it.

Makes 24

24 chicken drumsticks

1 teaspoon salt

½ teaspoon black pepper

1 cup honey

¼ cup chopped garlic

1 tablespoon hot pepper sauce

■ Preheat oven to 400 degrees F. Place drumsticks on 2 rimmed baking sheets that have been lined with aluminum foil; season with salt and pepper. Roast 30 minutes.

■ Meanwhile, in a medium bowl, combine honey, garlic, and hot pepper sauce.

■ After roasting for 30 minutes, drain off excess liquid and baste with sauce. Return to the oven for 20 to 25 minutes or until no pink remains, basting occasionally.

ALL-IN-ONE TURKEY DINNER

It's crazy to me that some people only eat turkey once a year, especially when so many of them eagerly wait for Thanksgiving to roll around. Since the most common excuse I hear is, "It's so much work!" I came up with this recipe that combines practically all of your favorite Thanksgiving dishes in one simple, slow cooker dinner. All that's missing are the mashed potatoes and gravy, but you can whip that up in no time!

Serves 4 to 6

1 (8-ounce) package stuffing cubes

½ cup hot water

2 tablespoons butter, softened

1 onion, chopped

1 (8-ounce) package sliced mushrooms

¼ cup dried cranberries

1 (3-pound) boneless turkey breast (see note)

½ teaspoon salt

½ teaspoon black pepper

6 carrots, cut into 1-inch chunks

- Coat a 3-½-quart or larger slow cooker with cooking spray.

- Place stuffing cubes in slow cooker and add water, butter, onion, mushrooms, and cranberries; mix well.

- Sprinkle turkey breast with salt and pepper and place it over stuffing mixture, then place carrots around turkey. Cover and cook on LOW 7 to 8 hours.

- Remove turkey to a cutting board; let rest 5 minutes before slicing. Remove carrots to a serving bowl. Stir stuffing and serve with turkey and carrots.

I find that most supermarkets carry bone-in turkey breasts. If you buy it this way, you can remove the bone at home by running a sharp knife between the meat and the bone and separating the two. You can also ask the butcher to de-bone a turkey breast for you. MCM

I'm the guy who can crave saucy barbecued ribs on a Wednesday and a fancy steak on a Saturday. As long as there's lots of flavor in the dish, I'm all in! MCM

BEEF & PORK

TRADITIONAL BEEF POT ROAST

Pot roasts have this magic quality of being able to bring families together. Everyone loves this comforting dish and most of us have grown up eating a version that's been passed down through the generations. Even though I grew up eating lots of rabbit roasts (yeah, that's the norm for the French!) I wanted to share this traditional beef pot roast that your family will love. It's a good one for starting new and tasty traditions with the people you love most.

Serves 5 to 6

1 tablespoon vegetable oil

1 (3-pound) boneless beef chuck roast

1 teaspoon salt

½ teaspoon black pepper

2 onions, coarsely chopped

1 cup dry red wine

2 sprigs fresh thyme

2 teaspoons chopped garlic

2 cups beef broth

1 bay leaf

3 large carrots, cut into 1-inch pieces

2 pounds potatoes, peeled and cut into 2-inch pieces

■ Preheat oven to 350 degrees F.

■ In a Dutch oven on the stovetop, heat oil over high heat until hot, but not smoking. Sprinkle roast with salt and pepper and place in Dutch oven. Cook 5 minutes, turning to brown on all sides, then remove from pot. Add onion and sauté 6 to 8 minutes, or until tender. Return roast to pot. Add wine, thyme, garlic, beef broth, and bay leaf; bring to a simmer.

■ Cover pot and transfer to oven to cook for 1 hour. Add carrots and potatoes. Cover and cook 35 to 40 minutes more, or until meat and veggies are fork tender. Remove bay leaf and discard. You can either cut up the roast or slice it across the grain depending on how "fall apart" tender it is. Serve with the vegetables and pan juices.

A Dutch oven is an oven-safe, heavy-duty pot. If you don't have one, you can brown the roast in a skillet and transfer it to a roasting pan before covering it and placing it in the oven. MCM

COUNTRY-FRIED STEAK WITH HOMEMADE GRAVY

I may not be a Southern guy, but when I make this dish I feel like turning on some country music and throwing on my cowboy boots. (Can you even imagine that?) The homemade milk gravy on top is the perfect finishing touch. Don't forget to set out a side of biscuits and mashed potatoes!

Serves 4

4 beef cubed steaks (1 to 1-¼ pounds total), pounded to ¼-inch thickness

¼ cup Worcestershire sauce

1 cup all-purpose flour

½ teaspoon salt

½ teaspoon black pepper

¾ cup buttermilk

½ cup vegetable oil

1-¼ cups milk

¼ cup chicken broth

- In a large resealable plastic bag, marinate the steaks in Worcestershire sauce for 30 minutes in the refrigerator.

- In a shallow dish, combine flour, salt, and pepper. Pour buttermilk into another shallow dish. Dip steaks in flour mixture, coating completely, then in buttermilk, and again in flour. Reserve remaining flour mixture.

- Meanwhile, in a large deep skillet over medium-high heat, heat oil until hot, but not smoking. Add steaks and cook 3 to 4 minutes per side, or until cooked through and coating is golden. Drain on a paper towel-lined platter and cover to keep warm.

- To make the gravy, add 1/3 cup of remaining flour mixture (yes, the leftover flour from breading the steaks) to skillet. Cook 2 to 3 minutes, or until flour is browned and mixed well with the pan drippings, stirring constantly. Slowly, whisk in milk and broth, stirring until thickened. If the gravy is too thick, feel free to add a little more milk until it's the right consistency. Serve gravy over steak.

THE FAMOUS BEEF BURGUNDY

The aromas of this hearty beef stew brings back childhood memories of delicious dinners. It makes me laugh to think that what I've always known as an everyday family favorite is now considered a fancy restaurant dish. To keep it traditional, my recipe calls for mushrooms, but when I make it for myself I leave them out, since I'm already a "fungi." (Plus, I'm allergic.)

Serves 5 to 6

1 teaspoon dried thyme

1 teaspoon black pepper

2 pounds boneless beef chuck, cut into 1-inch chunks

2 tablespoons vegetable oil

6 cups beef broth

1 cup Burgundy or other dry red wine

3 cloves garlic, minced

3 carrots, cut into 1-inch chunks

2 potatoes, peeled and cut into 1-inch chunks

½ pound fresh mushrooms, cut in half

1 onion, cut into 1-inch chunks

¼ cup water

2 tablespoons all-purpose flour

■ In a large bowl, combine thyme and pepper. Add beef and toss to coat.

■ In a large pot over medium heat, heat oil until hot, but not smoking; add beef and sauté 8 to 10 minutes or until browned, stirring occasionally. Add broth, wine, and garlic. Stir to remove all the bits of flavor that are stuck to the pot.

■ Reduce heat to low, cover, and simmer 45 minutes, stirring occasionally. Add carrots, potatoes, mushrooms, and onion; cover and cook 30 more minutes or until meat is tender, stirring occasionally.

■ In a small bowl, combine water and flour; gradually stir mixture into stew. Continue cooking, uncovered, about 5 more minutes, or until slightly thickened, stirring occasionally.

Since this stew is packed with so much flavor, I suggest serving it alongside some crusty bread. That way, you can sop up every last bit. MCM

DATE-NIGHT STEAKS WITH CREAM SAUCE

Technically, this is a recipe for "steak au poivre," which is basically a French-style, pepper-crusted steak. But, since I typically make this whenever I want to have a romantic night in, I like to call this my "Date-Night Steak." It's a nice dish to make at home together, whether it's because someone forgot to make dinner reservations or because you both could use a quiet night in. Serve with freshly roasted vegetables and a little wine to make it a really special meal.

Serves 2

1 tablespoon coarsely ground black pepper

2 (4-ounce, 1-inch thick) beef tenderloin steaks

1 tablespoon vegetable oil

2 tablespoons butter

¼ cup brandy

¼ cup beef broth

¼ teaspoon salt

½ teaspoon cornstarch

½ cup heavy cream

■ Preheat oven to 350 degrees F. Press pepper evenly onto both sides of steaks. Make sure you use coarsely ground pepper, so that every bite is full of crunch.

■ In a cast iron or oven-proof skillet over medium-high heat, heat oil until hot, but not smoking. Add steaks and sear until browned on each side. Place in oven 5 to 8 minutes, or until a meat thermometer inserted in center registers 135 degrees F, or to desired doneness beyond that. Let meat rest 5 minutes before serving, so all the juices seal in.

■ Meanwhile, in a medium skillet over medium heat, melt butter, then remove skillet from heat. Stir in brandy and place back on heat. In a small bowl, combine beef broth, salt, and cornstarch and stir until smooth. Whisk broth mixture into skillet. Stir in heavy cream and simmer 3 to 5 minutes, or until thickened. Serve sauce over steaks.

GARLIC AND LIME MARINATED STEAKS

An easy way to add flavor to meat is to let it marinate for a couple of hours (the longer the better!). This allows the marinade to really soak into the meat, making it even more tender and flavorful. My garlic and lime marinade, complete with plenty of fresh parsley, will add even more layers of flavor to your next steak dinner. It's sure to be a hit!

Serves 4 to 5

1 bunch fresh parsley, chopped (about 1 cup)

2 cups olive oil

¼ cup fresh lime juice

6 cloves garlic, chopped

1 teaspoon salt

½ teaspoon black pepper

2 to 2-½ pounds skirt steak

- In a medium bowl, combine all ingredients except steak; whisk until well combined. Set aside 1/2 cup.

- Place skirt steak in a resealable plastic bag along with the remaining marinade, leaving the 1/2 cup set aside; toss to coat. Marinate at least 2 hours in the refrigerator, or overnight.

- Remove steak from marinade; discard excess used marinade. Place steak in a preheated grill pan and cook 4 to 5 minutes per side, or to desired doneness. (I recommend not cooking this cut of meat past medium or it will start to get tough.)

- Remove steak to a cutting board; let rest 5 minutes before slicing thinly across the grain. Stir reserved marinade and spoon over sliced steak.

ALL-IN-ONE ASIAN STIR FRY

You'll find all your favorite Asian flavors in this easy recipe, including fresh ginger, snow peas, peppers, soy sauce, rice vinegar, and more. Best of all, this is another all-in-one meal that cooks up all in one skillet, so you don't have to worry about spending hours at the sink afterwards.

Serves 3 to 4

2 tablespoons peanut oil

6 to 8 slices fresh ginger

2 cloves garlic, minced

1 pound boneless top sirloin, thinly sliced across the grain

1 red bell pepper, thinly sliced

8 ounces fresh snow peas, trimmed

1 onion, cut into ½-inch wedges

2 tablespoons soy sauce

2 tablespoons rice vinegar

1 tablespoon light brown sugar

1 teaspoon cornstarch

4 cups hot cooked rice

■ In a wok or large nonstick skillet over high heat, heat oil until hot, but not smoking. Add ginger, garlic, and beef; stir frequently and cook 2 minutes, or until beef is browned. Add red pepper, snow peas, and onion, and continue cooking 2 to 3 minutes, or until vegetables are crisp-tender. You want to make sure you keep stirring this, that's why it's called a stir fry!

■ In a small bowl, whisk soy sauce, vinegar, brown sugar, and cornstarch. Pour into wok and cook until sauce thickens, tossing to coat. Serve over rice.

If you'd like to add an extra crunch, toss in a half cup or so of peanuts right before serving. MCM

HOMESTYLE MEATLOAF

There must be about a 101 different ways to make meatloaf these days. I've literally seen everything from a Tex-Mex version that's stuffed with salsa and beans, to a pizza-style version that calls for mozzarella cheese, oregano, and marinara sauce. While I'm sure many of these variations are tasty, I don't think you can ever go wrong with the traditional, homestyle version. After all, it's this American classic that has inspired the others.

Serves 4 to 6

1-½ pounds ground beef

3 slices white bread, torn into small pieces

1 onion, finely chopped

1 egg

¼ cup milk

½ teaspoon dry mustard

1 teaspoon salt

¼ teaspoon black pepper

3 tablespoons ketchup

■ Preheat oven to 350 degrees F.

■ In a large bowl, combine all ingredients except ketchup; mix well, but don't overmix or the meat will get tough. Gently press mixture evenly into a 9- x 5-inch loaf pan. Spoon ketchup over top.

■ Bake 60 to 65 minutes, or until no pink remains and juices run clear. Remove from oven; drain and allow to sit 5 minutes. Slice into 1-inch slices and dig in.

Since I love caramelized onions, I sometimes like to serve them on top of this meatloaf. To make them, just heat 2 tablespoons of vegetable oil in a large skillet over high heat. Once it's hot, add 3 large onions that have been cut in half and thinly sliced. Cook for 15 to 20 minutes, or until they're browned, stirring occasionally. Season with ¼ teaspoon of salt, ⅛ teaspoon of black pepper, and 1 tablespoon of brown sugar. Cook a couple more minutes and you're done! MCM

SATISFYING STUFFED CABBAGE

Now, I'm not Polish, but I'm pretty sure the only thing that could make this recipe more authentic-tasting is if it were served to you by a real Polish grandmother, or "babcia." In this recipe, you'll find true Old World comfort with a high dose of deliciousness. By stuffing cabbage leaves with a hearty helping of ground beef and rice, you can bet this meal will satisfy even the hungriest bellies at your dinner table.

Serves 5 to 6

1 large cabbage, cored

1 (28-ounce) can crushed tomatoes, undrained

2 tablespoons light brown sugar

1 tablespoon Worcestershire sauce

1 tablespoon lemon juice

1 pound ground beef

1 cup cooled cooked rice

1 onion, chopped

1 egg

1 teaspoon salt

½ teaspoon black pepper

■ Preheat oven to 350 degrees F. Coat a 9- x 13-inch baking dish with cooking spray.

■ In a large soup pot over high heat, bring 1-inch of water to a boil. Place cabbage in water, cored-side down; cover pot, and reduce heat to low. Steam 20 minutes, or until cabbage leaves pull apart easily. (Careful, the steam is very hot.) Drain and set aside.

■ In a medium bowl, combine tomatoes and their juice, brown sugar, Worcestershire sauce, and lemon juice; mix well and set aside. In a large bowl, combine remaining ingredients and 2 tablespoons tomato mixture; mix well.

■ Place 1 cup tomato mixture in bottom of baking dish. Peel a cabbage leaf off the head and remove the thick stem. Place about a ¼ cup of the meat mixture in center of leaf. Starting at core end, make a roll, folding over the sides and rolling loosely. Place seam-side down in baking dish; repeat with remaining cabbage leaves and meat mixture. Spoon remaining tomato mixture evenly over top of cabbage rolls and cover.

■ Bake 1-¼ hours. Uncover and cook 10 additional minutes, or until beef is no longer pink.

AMERICAN CHOP SUEY

Whether you grew up calling this "chop suey," "goulash," or "hot dish," isn't important. What's important is that you give this a try right now...or later on if you're reading this at breakfast. The beauty about this dish is that you can mix and match with whatever you've got in the fridge. Add more onion, leave out the peppers, use different cheeses, try with tomato sauce... you get the idea! Just make sure you don't leave out the beef and macaroni.

Serves 4 to 5

8 ounces elbow macaroni

1-½ pounds ground beef

½ green bell pepper, chopped

1 onion, chopped

1 (28-ounce) jar spaghetti sauce

1 teaspoon garlic powder

1 teaspoon salt

½ teaspoon black pepper

½ cup (2 ounces) shredded cheddar cheese

½ cup (2 ounces) shredded mozzarella cheese

■ Cook macaroni according to package directions; drain and cover to keep warm.

■ In a large skillet over high heat, brown the ground beef, bell pepper, and onion 6 to 8 minutes, or until no pink remains in the beef, stirring frequently. Drain off excess liquid.

■ Add macaroni, spaghetti sauce, garlic powder, salt, and black pepper; mix well. Reduce heat to medium-low and simmer 5 to 7 minutes, or until heated through. Sprinkle with cheeses, cover, and simmer about 1 minute, or until cheese is melted.

I like to use a blend of cheddar and mozzarella since the cheddar adds a bite and the mozzarella delivers a gooey cheesiness. And if you have some fresh basil in the fridge or in your garden, add slivers of that on top of the cheese before serving. MCM

FAMILY-SIZED PIZZA ROLL

You might want to bookmark this page for the next time your family asks for a pizza night. They'll love this rolled-up version of a traditional pie stuffed full of pepperoni, sausage, and plenty of cheese (go ahead and add more if you're a cheese fanatic like me!). It's a super simple dinner recipe that's ready in less time than it takes to have a pizza delivered.

Serves 5 to 6

1 (13.8-ounce) package refrigerated pizza dough

½ cup pizza sauce

½ cup pepperoni slices

1 cup pre-cooked sausage crumbles

½ teaspoon garlic powder

1 cup shredded mozzarella cheese

■ Preheat oven to 425 degrees F. Coat a baking sheet with cooking spray.

■ Unroll pizza crust dough on your counter top. Evenly spread pizza sauce over dough. Layer with pepperoni, sausage, garlic powder, and cheese. Starting with end of dough, roll up jelly roll-style and place on prepared baking sheet, seam-side down.

■ Bake 15 to 20 minutes, or until golden. Let rest 5 minutes, then slice and serve.

I like to sprinkle on some freshly grated Parmesan cheese right when it comes out of the oven. Oh, and don't forget to serve a crock or two of warmed pizza sauce for dunking!

MCM

MOUTHWATERING PATTY MELTS

Let's get one thing straight before I go on—a patty melt is not a hamburger! A patty melt is a sandwich that just so happens to be made with a delicious hamburger patty. And if the thought of one doesn't get your mouth watering, then I'm afraid I'm going to need you to take out a skillet and the ingredients for this recipe right now. From the toasted rye bread to the caramelized onions and cheesy goodness, this sandwich never disappoints.

Serves 2

2 tablespoons butter, divided

1 large onion, thinly sliced

¾ pound ground beef

Pinch of salt and pepper

4 slices rye bread

4 slices Gouda cheese

¼ cup Thousand Island dressing

- In a large skillet or griddle over medium-high heat, melt 1 tablespoon butter; sauté onion 6 to 8 minutes, or until it starts to brown. Remove to a bowl and cover to keep warm.

- Form the ground beef into 2 equal-sized patties; sprinkle with salt and pepper. In the same skillet over medium-high heat, cook patties 5 to 6 minutes per side, until no longer pink in center, or until desired doneness. Remove from skillet and keep warm.

- Spread remaining 1 tablespoon of butter over 1 side of each slice of bread. Place in skillet buttered-side down. Top each with a slice of cheese, and heat until cheese is melted and bread is golden.

- To assemble, place a burger patty on top of melted cheese on 2 of the slices of bread; top with onions and dressing. Place the other 2 slices of bread with melted cheese on top. Serve immediately.

If you want to make a bunch of these, the recipe is certainly easy enough to multiply. The secret to keeping these warm while making the rest is to place them on a baking sheet and pop them in a low oven (250 degrees F) for 5 to 10 minutes. This way, the cheese really melts and everything stays toasty hot. MCM

SWEET AND TANGY PORK CHOPS

You'll be licking your chops after a taste of these chops! They're made from the perfect combination of sweet and tangy ingredients (although you might not want to tell your family one of those ingredients is prunes until after they've taken a bite and said "yum!"). Tender and tasty, these foolproof chops go well with just about any of your favorite side dishes.

Serves 4

1 tablespoon vegetable oil

4 (1-inch-thick) boneless pork chops (about 2 pounds)

½ teaspoon salt

½ teaspoon black pepper

½ cup pitted prunes, sliced

½ cup dried apricots, sliced

1 onion, thinly sliced

½ cup apple juice

2 tablespoons brown sugar

2 tablespoons cider vinegar

■ In a large skillet over medium-high heat, heat oil until hot, but not smoking. Sprinkle pork chops with salt and pepper. Sear pork chops about 5 minutes on each side, or until browned; drain.

■ Add remaining ingredients to skillet. Cover, reduce heat to low and simmer 15 to 20 minutes, or until desired doneness, stirring occasionally.

BETTER-THAN-EVER BARBECUED RIBS

What makes these "better-than-ever"? The fact that these ribs cook all day long in the slow cooker, so you can get them ready at the start of your day and by dinnertime they'll be ready, and your house will smell heavenly. Plus, slow cooking your ribs makes them extra tender and even more flavor packed. This is a great dinner to kick off the weekend—you won't even mind that it's a little goopy and messy!

Serves 4 to 5

1-½ cups ketchup

½ cup brown sugar

3 tablespoons white vinegar

3 tablespoons Worcestershire sauce

2 tablespoons yellow mustard

⅓ cup finely chopped onion

1 teaspoon garlic powder

1 teaspoon salt

½ teaspoon black pepper

4 pounds baby back ribs, cut into individual ribs

■ In a medium bowl, combine ketchup, brown sugar, vinegar, Worcestershire sauce, mustard, and onion; mix well and set aside.

■ In a small bowl, combine garlic powder, salt, and pepper; mix well. Before seasoning, try to remove the thin silver skin from the ribs by gently pulling it off. It might give you a bit of a fight, but, if you can remove it, it will make your ribs more tender. Then, using your hands, rub the seasoning mixture over the ribs, coating thoroughly.

■ Place ribs in a 5-quart or larger slow cooker and pour sauce over ribs. Cover and cook on LOW 7 to 8 hours, or until ribs are fork-tender. (While they cook, I'll make a few side dishes, maybe take a nap, or get ready for my next airing on QVC.) When done, I serve them smothered in the sauce.

If you don't have all day to wait for these, you can cook these on HIGH and they'll be ready in about 4 to 5 hours. MCM

PORK TENDERLOIN IN MARSALA SAUCE

I may not be able to enjoy this dish myself (oh, mushroom allergies!), but I've made it for company on quite a few occasions and have received rave reviews. The most important part to making a perfect pork tenderloin is not to overcook it. No one wants a slice of shoe leather on their plate! Instead, cook it till medium, so that it stays juicy. Then, top it with my wonderful Marsala sauce and enjoy every last bite.

Serves 3 to 4

2 tablespoons all-purpose flour

½ teaspoon salt

⅛ teaspoon black pepper

1 (14- to 16-ounce) pork tenderloin

3 tablespoons olive oil

½ pound sliced fresh mushrooms

2 onions, thinly sliced

½ cup sweet Marsala wine

■ In a shallow dish, combine flour, salt, and pepper; mix well. Coat pork tenderloin with mixture.

■ In a large skillet or Dutch oven over medium-high heat, heat oil until hot, but not smoking. Add tenderloin and cook 6 to 8 minutes, turning to brown on all sides; remove to a platter and set aside. Add mushrooms and onions to skillet and sauté 6 to 8 minutes, or until tender, stirring occasionally; stir in wine.

■ Return tenderloin to skillet and cook 5 to 6 minutes, or until internal temperature reaches 145 degrees F for medium, or to desired doneness beyond that. Remember, you want to keep it juicy!

■ Slice tenderloin and serve topped with Marsala sauce.

Marsala wine can be found either sweet or dry. For this recipe I prefer the sweet kind as it adds a rich, caramelized flavor that's incredible. Once you try cooking with it, you're going to fall in love with it. MCM

GERMAN ONE-POT COUNTRY-STYLE RIBS

I don't think it gets any easier than this. All you need are four ingredients and one pot to pull off this mouthwatering main dish. It's pretty much a dump and roast type of recipe! Oh, and if you don't think you're going to like the sauerkraut, I'm begging you not to knock it until you try it here. I've been told this recipe can perform taste bud miracles.

Serves 3 to 4

1 (2-pound) package refrigerated sauerkraut, rinsed and drained

1 (3-pound) package pork country-style ribs

1 (1-ounce) envelope onion soup mix

1 onion, thinly sliced

▪ Preheat oven to 350 degrees F. Coat a 3-quart or larger covered baking dish with cooking spray.

▪ Place sauerkraut in baking dish. Place ribs over sauerkraut, sprinkle with soup mix, then top with onion. If you don't have a covered baker, use a 9- x13-inch pan and cover it with foil.

▪ Roast 1-1/2 hours. Uncover and continue cooking for an additional 15 minutes or so, until they're fall-off-the-bone tender. Serve ribs smothered in the sauerkraut.

If you're not having fun in the kitchen, then you're not doing it right. I'm not above getting a little goofy at times; it's what keeps me sane when I've got lots of food to prepare! MCM

SEAFOOD, PASTA, & MORE

EXTRA-SAUCY FRIED BUFFALO SHRIMP

I hope you like things a little spicy because these shrimp are twice-coated in a kicked-up, seasoned flour mixture before they're sent to the frying pan. And that's not all! I toss them in plenty of Buffalo sauce to add even more flavor and heat. Make no bones about it, nothing compares to these crispy and saucy shrimp.

Serves 4 to 6

¾ cup all-purpose flour

1 tablespoon baking powder

1 teaspoon salt

½ teaspoon cayenne pepper

2 eggs

¼ cup milk

½ cup vegetable oil

1-½ pounds large shrimp, peeled and deveined, with tails left on

½ stick butter

¼ cup cayenne pepper sauce (wing sauce)

Blue cheese dressing

Celery sticks

■ In a shallow dish, combine flour, baking powder, salt, and cayenne pepper; mix well. In another shallow dish, beat eggs and milk with a fork until well combined.

■ In a large skillet over medium-high heat, heat oil until hot, but not smoking.

■ Dip the shrimp in flour mixture, then egg mixture, and then back in flour mixture, until completely coated. Cook shrimp 2 to 3 minutes per side, or until golden. Drain on a paper towel-lined platter.

■ In a microwave-safe bowl, melt butter in microwave. Stir in cayenne pepper sauce.

■ Place shrimp in a bowl, pour the sauce over shrimp, and toss to coat. Just like Buffalo wings, serve these with blue cheese dressing, celery and lots of napkins.

Try not to make the same mistake I did the first time I made these! I used Tabasco® sauce instead of cayenne pepper sauce (wing sauce) and ended up with one fiery hot dish.

MCM

HINT-OF-LIME COCONUT SHRIMP

Regular coconut shrimp are good, but my extra-crispy coconut shrimp are phenomenal. I add a little lime juice to the coating, which adds even more tropical taste to the shrimp. Fried until they're golden on the outside and succulent on the inside, these shrimp have never failed to impress anyone I've shared them with.

Serves 3 to 4

½ cup all-purpose flour

1 tablespoon sugar

1 teaspoon cayenne pepper (optional)

½ teaspoon salt

2 eggs

2 tablespoons lime juice

1-½ cups sweetened flaked coconut

¾ cup Panko bread crumbs

1 pound large shrimp, peeled and deveined, with tails left on

2 cups vegetable oil

- ■ In a shallow dish, combine flour, sugar, cayenne pepper, if desired, and salt; mix well. In a medium bowl, beat together the eggs and lime juice. Combine coconut and bread crumbs in another shallow dish.

- ■ Coat shrimp with flour mixture, then with egg mixture. Roll in coconut mixture, pressing coconut firmly onto shrimp to coat completely.

- ■ In a large saucepan over medium heat, heat oil until hot, but not smoking. Cook shrimp in batches for about 2 minutes, turning once during cooking. Remove shrimp when golden and cooked through. Drain on a paper towel-lined platter. Serve immediately.

I'm a big dipper—no, not like the kind in the solar system. What I mean is that I'm a person who likes to dip all sorts of things in a variety of sauces. For these, I break out the sweet and sour sauce, spicy mustard, and plum sauce. Hey, you've got to have options!

MCM

MEDITERRANEAN SHRIMP 'N' SHELLS

When you sauté shrimp in garlic and butter, you better believe your house is going to smell like heaven! Add in all of the fresh flavors of the Mediterranean, like spinach, tomatoes, pine nuts (I love the crunch!), and lemon juice, and it gets even better. Served over your favorite pasta, this makes for one tasty and surprisingly quick dinner.

Serves 4 to 5

1 pound medium-sized pasta shells (see note)

1 stick butter

1 pound medium shrimp, peeled and deveined, with tails removed

1 tablespoon chopped fresh garlic

½ teaspoon salt

½ teaspoon black pepper

1 (6-ounce) bag fresh baby spinach

½ pint cherry tomatoes, halved

¼ cup pine nuts

1 tablespoon fresh lemon juice (juice of ½ lemon)

■ Cook pasta according to package directions; drain and keep warm in a serving bowl.

■ Meanwhile, in a large skillet over medium-high heat, melt butter; add shrimp, garlic, salt, and pepper, and sauté 2 to 3 minutes, or until shrimp turn pink, stirring occasionally. Remove shrimp mixture to a bowl.

■ Add spinach, cherry tomatoes, and pine nuts to skillet and cook 2 to 3 minutes, or until spinach is wilted. Return shrimp mixture to skillet, toss to coat, and simmer until heated through. Serve over the pasta and drizzle with lemon juice.

Shell-shaped pasta is typically sold in three different sizes: Usually, the smaller ones are used for soups, the medium-sized in salads (and in recipes like this), and the jumbo-sized ones are best for stuffing. MCM

MARINATED SHRIMP SKEWERS

These shrimp are all lined up and ready to go one-by-one right into your mouth. Marinated in a sweet chili sauce that has just the right amount of tang to it, these shrimp are bursting with flavor. I think they're just what you need at your next cookout. Or, if you can't wait, just make them at home on a grill pan!

Serves 4 to 5

½ cup chili sauce

⅓ cup olive oil

2 tablespoons red wine vinegar

4 cloves garlic, minced

2 tablespoons chopped fresh cilantro

½ teaspoon salt

¼ teaspoon cayenne pepper

1-½ pounds large shrimp, peeled and deveined, with tails left on

Skewers (see note)

■ In a resealable plastic bag, combine chili sauce, oil, vinegar, garlic, cilantro, salt, and cayenne pepper; mix well. Add shrimp and toss gently until evenly coated. Cover and refrigerate 1 to 2 hours.

■ Right before you're ready to serve, lightly coat a grill rack with cooking spray, and preheat grill to medium-high heat.

■ Thread shrimp onto skewers, discarding excess marinade. Cook shrimp 2 to 3 minutes per side, or until pink.

If you're planning on using wooden skewers, make sure you soak them in water for 10 to 15 minutes before skewering the shrimp, so they won't burn on the grill. MCM

BRONZED SCALLOPS WITH LEMON-BUTTER LINGUINE

I hate it when you order scallops at a restaurant and the waiter brings you a plate of chewy rubber balls! It isn't hard to keep your scallops plump and juicy. All you've got to do is to dry them really well before searing them, like I tell you to do in this recipe. Once you've got perfectly cooked scallops, you can add them to just about anything to take dinner to the next level. Here, a lemon-butter linguine is the perfect fit!

Serves 4 to 5

1-¼ sticks butter, divided

2 tablespoons olive oil

1-½ pounds sea scallops

½ teaspoon salt, plus extra for sprinkling

¼ teaspoon black pepper, plus extra for sprinkling

Paprika for sprinkling

½ cup finely chopped onion

1 cup white wine

2 tablespoons fresh lemon juice

2 tablespoons chopped fresh parsley

2 teaspoons lemon zest

½ pound linguine, cooked according to package directions

■ In a large skillet over medium-high heat, melt 2 tablespoons butter with oil until hot. Pat scallops dry with paper towel (this is important!) and sprinkle both sides with salt, pepper, and paprika. Place in skillet and sear 2 to 3 minutes per side, or until browned. Remove to a plate.

■ In the same skillet over medium heat, melt remaining 1 stick butter; sauté onion 3 to 4 minutes, or until tender. Stir in wine, lemon juice, parsley, ½ teaspoon salt, and ¼ teaspoon pepper and heat until hot, but do not brown, stirring occasionally.

■ Add scallops back to skillet and heat just until hot. Sprinkle with lemon zest and toss with warm pasta.

"CRABMEAT" FISH ROLLUPS

You might start considering yourself a "real" chef once you make this recipe—I know I did the first time I made it! Who would've thought that it'd be this easy to pull off something that looks as gourmet as it tastes? Even my family was impressed by all the "hard work" I had put into that week's "Fish Friday" dinner. (There may or may not have been some embellishing about what was involved.)

Serves 4

½ pound imitation crabmeat, flaked

½ cup seasoned bread crumbs

1 celery stalk, finely chopped

3 tablespoons mayonnaise

1 teaspoon Worcestershire sauce

½ teaspoon onion powder

½ teaspoon black pepper

4 white-fleshed fish fillets, such as flounder or tilapia (about 1-½ pounds)

2 tablespoons butter, melted

¼ teaspoon paprika

■ Preheat oven to 375 degrees F. Coat a 9- x 13-inch baking dish with cooking spray.

■ In a medium bowl, combine crabmeat, bread crumbs, celery, mayonnaise, Worcestershire sauce, onion powder, and pepper; mix well.

■ Place fish fillets on a cutting board. Spread crabmeat mixture over each fillet, dividing evenly, and roll up jelly-roll style. Place seam side down in baking dish. Drizzle with melted butter and sprinkle with paprika.

■ Bake 25 to 30 minutes, or until fish flakes easily with a fork. Serve immediately.

If you want to get all fancy, you can always use real crabmeat. It's a bit pricey, but a welcome swap. MCM

CLAMS SCAMPI WITH DUNKIN' BREAD

I'm going to save you the trouble of packing your bags and heading to the shore for a taste of great seafood (you can thank me later!). Instead, you can just make these clams on your stovetop. They're cooked scampi-style, which means there's lots of butter and garlic in the sauce (has your mouth started to water yet?). The bread, of course, is for dunking and sopping up every last bit.

Serves 2

½ cup white wine

⅓ cup water

3 cloves garlic, minced

2 teaspoons chopped fresh parsley

2 dozen raw littleneck clams in shell

½ lemon, cut into wedges

½ stick butter

Toasted French bread, for dunking

■ In a large steamer, soup pot, or my 4th Burner Pot (Pictured-yes, it's the one you see me selling on QVC!) over high heat, bring wine, water, garlic, and parsley to a boil.

■ Place clams and lemon in steamer basket or directly in pot and steam, covered, 8 to 10 minutes, or until clams open on their own. Remove basket and discard any unopened clams.

■ Add butter to broth mixture and heat until butter melts. Place clams in serving bowl, pour broth over them and serve with toasted French bread.

PUB-STYLE FRIED FISH

About four times a year I travel to London to visit QVC's UK studios. While I'm there, I like to drop in to one of my favorite pubs for a pint and a classic English meal of fish and chips. Now, this recipe may not be exactly how they make it across the pond, but I can promise you that the beer batter I use to coat the fish is really tasty. As for the "chips," be sure to check out page 160 for the recipe!

Serves 4

1-½ cups pancake mix

1 tablespoon sugar

½ teaspoon salt

½ teaspoon cayenne pepper

¾ cup beer

1 egg

2 tablespoons all-purpose flour

Peanut oil for frying

2-½ pounds white-fleshed fish, cut into 4 fillets (cod or haddock)

■ In a large bowl, combine pancake mix, sugar, salt, cayenne pepper, beer, and egg; mix well. (You can use any beer you prefer, but I found that a light ale adds just the right malty flavor.) Place flour in a shallow dish.

■ In a large deep skillet over medium heat, heat 1 inch of oil until hot, but not smoking.

■ Coat fish evenly in flour then dip into batter, coating completely. Fry 3 to 5 minutes per side, or until coating is golden and fish flakes easily with a fork. Drain on a paper towel-lined platter. Serve immediately.

Whenever I pan fry, I always play it safe by making sure the pan is deep enough, so that oil doesn't splatter all over the stove. Besides being safer, it makes it a whole lot easier to clean up. If you don't have a deep skillet, a soup pot works, too. MCM

SALMON PATTY SANDWICHES

Burgers are great, but every once in a while it's nice to have something a little different. That's why I'm going to help you lure your family to the dinner table with this simple salmon recipe. All you need are some basic ingredients and about a pound of fresh salmon fillets. Set out a few of their favorite sandwich toppings (I'm thinking some shredded romaine and tomato slices) and let them put on their own finishing touches.

Serves 4

1 pound skinless salmon fillets, cut into 1-inch chunks

1 to 2 slices fresh white bread

2 scallions, cut into 1-inch pieces

1 tablespoon lemon juice

1 tablespoon chopped fresh dill

¼ teaspoon salt

¼ teaspoon black pepper

4 kaiser rolls, split

■ Place all ingredients except rolls in a food processor; pulse until coarsely chopped and well combined. (You may need to scrape down the sides.) With your hands, form salmon mixture into 4 equal-sized patties.

■ Coat a large skillet with cooking spray. Cook patties over medium-high heat 3 to 4 minutes per side, or until cooked through. Place on rolls and serve.

These are great with a homemade dill sauce. To make it, just combine a ½ cup of mayo, ¼ cup of sour cream, 2 tablespoons of fresh chopped dill, a ½ teaspoon of lemon juice and a pinch each of salt, pepper, and onion powder. MCM

MAPLE-GLAZED BAKED SALMON

I'm going to be up front with you—it's worth it to splurge on real maple syrup for this recipe. The simple, 5-ingredient glaze just tastes so much better when you use the real stuff. Besides, now that you've read this, there's no fooling your mind with the imitation kind. I'm only looking out for your taste buds' best interests!

Serves 4

½ cup maple syrup

3 tablespoons soy sauce

1 clove garlic, minced

¼ teaspoon black pepper

2 scallions, sliced

4 (4-ounce) salmon fillets

■ In a large resealable plastic bag, combine syrup, soy sauce, garlic, pepper, and scallions; mix well. Place salmon in bag and marinate in refrigerator at least 2 hours, or overnight.

■ Preheat oven to 375 degrees F. Line a baking sheet with foil (If you skip this step you'll have to soak your baking sheet for a while to get the sticky glaze off.) and coat with cooking spray. Place salmon on baking sheet and drizzle with ¼ cup marinade. Discard excess marinade.

■ Bake 15 to 20 minutes, or until fish flakes easily. The baking time may vary greatly based on how thick the salmon is. If you are cooking the tail end, which is often thinner, you may want to check it after 10 minutes or so.

DAD'S BEST MAC 'N' CHEESE

When my kids come over for dinner, this is the one dish they always beg me to make. I hate to brag, but my mac 'n' cheese is awesome. I think that what makes it so good is that it's made with a blend of three cheeses. You get the sharp flavor from the cheddar, the smokiness from the Gouda, and the gooiness from the mozzarella. I can tell you right now, this one will have everyone doing the "happy dance, happy dance!"

Serves 6 to 8

1 pound elbow macaroni

1 stick plus 2 tablespoons butter, divided

½ cup all-purpose flour

1 teaspoon salt

½ teaspoon black pepper

3-½ cups milk

2 cups shredded sharp cheddar cheese

½ pound (2 cups) Gouda cheese, shredded

2 teaspoons Dijon mustard

½ pound mozzarella cheese, cut into 1-inch cubes

1 cup coarsely crushed saltine crackers

■ Preheat oven to 375 degrees F. Coat a 9- x 13-inch baking dish with cooking spray. In a large pot, cook macaroni according to package directions; drain and set aside.

■ Meanwhile, in the same pot over medium heat, melt 1 stick butter. Add flour, salt, and pepper; mix well. Gradually add milk, bring to a boil, and cook until smooth and thickened, stirring constantly. Add cheddar, Gouda, and mustard; continue stirring until melted. Remove from heat; add macaroni, and mix until evenly coated. Stir in mozzarella. Spoon mixture into baking dish.

■ In a microwave-safe bowl, melt remaining 2 tablespoons butter in microwave. Stir in crushed crackers; mix well. Sprinkle evenly over top of macaroni.

■ Bake uncovered 35 to 40 minutes, or until the top is golden and it's bubbling hot.

WEEKNIGHT TUNA NOODLE CASSEROLE

I didn't grow up eating this as a kid, but once I had kids of my own I learned that a tuna casserole can be a real lifesaver on busy weeknights. Not only is this made with stuff that most people always have stocked in their pantry, but you can basically throw everything together without doing a whole lot of work. Plus, it's comforting in a way that a TV dinner will never be.

Serves 4 to 5

1 (12-ounce) package medium egg noodles

2 (10-¾-ounce) cans condensed cream of mushroom soup

1-½ cups milk

1 (12-ounce) can chunk tuna, drained and flaked

2 cups frozen mixed vegetables

3 tablespoons butter, melted

½ teaspoon salt

½ teaspoon black pepper

1 cup coarsely crushed potato chips

- Cook noodles according to package directions; drain.

- Preheat oven to 350 degrees F. Coat a 2-½-quart or larger casserole dish with cooking spray.

- In a large bowl, combine soup and milk; mix well. Add noodles, tuna, mixed vegetables, butter, salt, and pepper. Pour mixture into casserole dish; top with potato chips.

- Bake 30 to 35 minutes, or until bubbling hot and the top is golden. Serve immediately.

ITALIAN SAUSAGE SHORTCUT LASAGNA

Homemade lasagna isn't usually the easiest thing to make for dinner, but it tastes so good I had to find a way to make it work for you. Now, I'm happy to introduce to you shortcut lasagna that's loaded with flavor. There's no precooking the noodles or making your own spaghetti sauce in this one. All it takes is a few simple steps and some oven time before you get to feast!

Serves 6 to 8

1 pound Italian sausage, casing removed

1 (15-ounce) container ricotta cheese

1 egg

3 cups shredded mozzarella cheese, divided

2 tablespoons chopped fresh basil

1 (24-ounce) jar spaghetti sauce

½ pound uncooked lasagna noodles (½ of a 16-ounce box)

1-½ cups diced zucchini

1 cup water

2 tablespoons Parmesan cheese

■ Preheat oven to 350 degrees F. Coat a 9- x 13-inch baking dish with cooking spray.

■ In a skillet over medium-high heat, cook sausage 8 to 10 minutes, or until browned and crumbled; drain and set aside.

■ In a medium bowl, combine ricotta cheese, egg, 1 cup shredded mozzarella, and the basil; set aside.

■ Pour half the spaghetti sauce into baking dish. Cover sauce with half the uncooked noodles; spread cheese mixture over noodles, then top with the sausage, zucchini, 1 cup shredded mozzarella, remaining noodles, and remaining sauce. Pour ¼ cup of water into each corner of baking dish. Cover tightly with aluminum foil.

■ Bake 1-¼ hours. Now here's the hard part, don't uncover the lasagna to peek at it while it's baking! (The steam that builds up inside the pan is what makes the noodles cook perfectly.) Remove from oven, uncover, and top with remaining 1 cup mozzarella and the Parmesan; bake 8 to 10 additional minutes, or until cheese is melted. Let rest 10 minutes before serving.

TOMATO-BASIL LINGUINE TOSS

Have you ever thought of starting your own garden? You might consider it once you've had a bite of this summertime-fresh pasta dish. It tastes best when you use really ripe tomatoes and freshly picked basil. The creaminess of the brie is what brings it all together, so if the only way you've ever eaten it is with crackers and fruit, then you're in for a delicious awakening.

Serves 4 to 5

1 pound linguine

½ cup olive oil

1 (8-ounce) brie cheese round, cut into ½-inch cubes

3 large ripe tomatoes, cut into 1-inch chunks

½ cup fresh basil leaves, thinly sliced

3 cloves garlic, minced

½ teaspoon salt

¼ teaspoon black pepper

Grated Parmesan cheese for sprinkling

■ Cook linguine according to package directions; drain well.

■ Meanwhile, in a large bowl, combine oil, brie, tomatoes, basil, garlic, salt, and pepper; mix well.

■ Add pasta to the tomato and cheese mixture and toss until well combined. Sprinkle with Parmesan cheese and serve warm.

HAM & PINEAPPLE DEEP DISH PIZZA

The sweetness from the pineapple, the saltiness from the ham; these are the things that I love about a classic Hawaiian pizza. But, you know me, I like to make everything a little bit better, so when I make this traditional favorite at home, I use barbecue sauce instead of tomato sauce for a tangy twist. Oh, and I make mine a deep dish, so that there's more room for toppings!

Serves 6

1 pound store-bought pizza dough

½ cup barbecue sauce

1-½ cups (6 ounces) shredded mozzarella cheese, divided

½ cup diced ham

1 (8-ounce) can pineapple tidbits, drained well

1 tablespoon chopped red onion (optional)

■ Preheat oven to 450 degrees F. Coat a 12-inch deep-dish pizza pan with cooking spray.

■ Using your fingertips or the heel of your hand, spread dough so it covers bottom of pan and comes ¾ of the way up the sides. Spread barbecue sauce over dough; sprinkle with ¾ cup cheese. Top with ham, pineapple, onion, if desired, and remaining ¾ cup cheese.

■ Bake 20 to 25 minutes, or until crust is crisp and brown. Let rest 5 minutes before cutting into wedges.

EGGPLANT ROLLATINI WITH PROSCIUTTO

You can still satisfy your cravings for Italian food without loading up your plate with pasta. Eggplant rollatini is one of my favorite, non-pasta, Italian dishes. It's simply eggplant that's rolled up with lots of creamy ricotta and, in my version, some sliced prosciutto. Pop it in the oven, top with your favorite spaghetti sauce and some mozzarella cheese, and enjoy your feast!

Serves 4 to 6

1 eggplant

2 eggs

1-½ cups Italian bread crumbs

2/3 cup olive oil

1-½ cups ricotta cheese

½ teaspoon garlic powder

10 slices prosciutto

2 cups spaghetti sauce

2 cups shredded mozzarella cheese

- Peel eggplant and cut lengthwise (not sliced into circles) into ¼-inch thick slices.

- Place eggs in a shallow dish and beat. Place bread crumbs in another shallow dish. (Pie plates work great for this.) Dip eggplant slices in egg, then evenly coat with bread crumbs.

- Heat about 2 tablespoons oil in a large skillet over medium-high heat. Fry eggplant on each side until golden brown. Remove to a paper towel-lined plate. Repeat with remaining oil and eggplant.

- Preheat the oven to 375 degrees F. In a small bowl, mix ricotta cheese and garlic powder, and spread mixture evenly onto breaded eggplant. Place a slice of prosciutto on top of each piece. (If you have any left, it's great for nibbling!) Roll up jelly roll-style, and place seam-side down in a 9- x 13-inch baking dish. Pour spaghetti sauce over the rolls, and top with mozzarella.

- Bake 15 to 20 minutes, or until heated through and the cheese is melted.

I'm not really a huge fan of "less is more." You know what's more? More! And that's sort of my philosophy when it comes to side dishes. The more side dish options I have, the happier I am. MCM

SIDE DISHES

SHORTCUT POTATO PANCAKES

These go great with a nice piece of fish. I mean, they're good no matter what you serve them next to, but I really like them with salmon or as an alternative to "chips" in a recipe for fish and chips. Since they start with shortcut potatoes, there's no need to hand grate them. Oh, and you'll notice that my recipe calls for Gouda cheese. That's because I think the cheese makes them even more irresistible.

Makes 12 to 14

1 (20-ounce) bag refrigerated shredded potatoes

4 ounces Gouda cheese, shredded

1 small onion, chopped

1 egg, beaten

¾ cup all-purpose flour

1 teaspoon salt

½ teaspoon black pepper

1 cup vegetable oil

■ In a large bowl, combine potatoes, cheese, onion, and egg; mix well. Add flour, salt, and pepper; mix until well combined. (If the mixture seems a bit dry, feel free to add a tablespoon or so of water.)

■ Using a ¼ cup measuring cup, scoop potato mixture and form into a pancake. Place these on a baking sheet and refrigerate until the oil is preheated as directed below.

■ In a large deep skillet over medium heat, heat oil until hot, but not smoking. Place pancakes in oil in batches, and cook 3 to 4 minutes per side, or until golden on both sides. Drain on a wire rack over a baking sheet. Serve immediately or reheat in a 300 degree oven when ready to serve.

If you're going to make these with fresh potatoes you're going to need about 3-½ cups, shredded. MCM

DIJON ROASTED POTATOES

Roasted potatoes are good on their own, but roast them with aromatic onion and garlic and you've already taken them to the next level. And, if that's not enough, the zing of Dijon mustard paired with fresh parsley will really kick things up another notch. Trust me, this one's a real winner.

Serves 4 to 6

2 pounds red-skinned potatoes, cut into quarters

2 onions, cut into quarters

4 cloves garlic, coarsely chopped

⅔ cup Dijon mustard

½ stick butter, melted

2 tablespoons chopped fresh parsley

■ Preheat oven to 350 degrees F. Coat a roasting pan with cooking spray.

■ Place potatoes, onions, and garlic in roasting pan; cover tightly with foil. Bake 50 to 60 minutes, or until potatoes are just fork-tender.

■ In a medium bowl, combine mustard, butter, and parsley; toss with hot potatoes.

■ Bake, uncovered, an additional 15 minutes, or until potatoes begin to turn golden and the edges get crispy. Serve piping hot.

Want to add another layer of awesomeness? Add a tablespoon of white horseradish to the mustard mixture before tossing it with the potatoes. MCM

CHEESY HASH BROWN CASSEROLE

Did you know that this dish is known as "Funeral Potatoes" in some parts of the country? The first time I heard that I have to admit that I was a little concerned. Lucky for all of us, there's nothing deadly about this cheesy hash brown casserole. It got its nickname after becoming the traditional dish to bring to a funeral in the Midwest. As it turns out, this casserole is the king of comforting side dishes.

Serves 6 to 8

1 stick butter, divided

½ cup diced onion

1 (32-ounce) package frozen shredded hash browns, thawed

2 cups shredded sharp cheddar cheese

1 (10-½-ounce) can cream of celery soup

2 cups sour cream

½ teaspoon salt

¼ teaspoon black pepper

1 cup coarsely crushed butter-flavored crackers

■ Preheat oven to 375 degrees F. Coat a 2-quart casserole or 9- x 13-inch baking dish with cooking spray.

■ In a small skillet over medium heat, melt ½ stick butter. Add onion and sauté 4 to 5 minutes, or until tender.

■ In a large bowl, combine hash browns, cheese, soup, sour cream, salt, pepper, and cooked onion; mix well. Spoon mixture into baking dish.

■ In a small microwave-safe bowl, melt remaining ½ stick butter in microwave; stir in crushed crackers. Sprinkle cracker mixture over potatoes. Cover baking dish with foil and bake 35 minutes. Remove foil and bake 10 to 15 additional minutes, or until golden brown and heated through.

HOMEMADE FRENCH FRIES

I'm a French fry fan, and no, I don't think it has anything to do with being French (although nothing beats a side of "pommes frites" with a steak au poivre). These are so simple, you don't even have to bother peeling the potatoes. Actually, leaving the skin on gives them a great rustic look, and when they get extra crispy...man are these good!

Serves 4 to 6

4 large Russet potatoes with skin on, cut lengthwise into ¼-inch-thick fries

2 cups ice cubes

3 cups vegetable oil

Salt for sprinkling

■ Place cut potatoes in a large bowl and cover with water. Place ice on top of potatoes; let sit 30 minutes. (Soaking the potatoes in ice water before frying them will make them extra crispy.)

■ In a soup pot over medium heat, heat oil to 350 degrees F. (To measure the temperature, you can use an inexpensive instant-read or meat thermometer or if you have a deep fryer, this would be a great time to dig it out.)

■ Drain potatoes and place on paper towels; pat dry. Don't skip this step; the potatoes need to be dry. Carefully place potatoes in oil and cook 15 to 20 minutes, or until golden brown, turning occasionally. Using a slotted spoon, remove fries to a paper towel-lined plate. Season with salt and serve.

Yeah, you could dip these into ketchup...or you can try my special French fry sauce. To make it, in a small bowl, combine 1/2 cup mayonnaise, 1/4 cup Dijon mustard, 1 teaspoon Worcestershire sauce, and 1 tablespoon minced chives. Mix it all up and refrigerate until you're ready to serve. Then, dip away! MCM

APRICOT-STUDDED CORNBREAD STUFFING

Chances are, no one in your family makes their stuffing this way, which means you've got a chance to introduce them to something new and mouthwatering. Once they get a taste of this savory and sweet stuffing, you'll be the one reaping all the compliments around the dinner table. So, invite the whole family over, and serve it next to your favorite roasted chicken or turkey.

Serves 6 to 8

1 stick butter

½ cup chopped onion

½ cup chopped celery

4 cornbread muffins

10 slices white bread

1-½ teaspoons poultry seasoning

2 teaspoons sugar

1 teaspoon salt

½ teaspoon black pepper

2 eggs, lightly beaten

1-½ cups chicken stock

½ cup dried apricots, chopped

■ Preheat oven to 350 degrees F. Coat a 2-quart casserole dish with cooking spray.

■ In a large skillet over medium heat, melt butter; sauté onion and celery 6 to 8 minutes, or until tender.

■ In a food processor, combine muffins and bread; pulse until crumbled. (You want this to be a coarse crumb, to keep the stuffing light and airy.) Place in a large bowl and add remaining ingredients, including sautéed vegetables; mix well. Place in baking dish and cover. If your baking dish does not have a cover, use foil.

■ Bake 30 minutes, then uncover and bake 20 to 25 more minutes, or until heated through and the top starts to get crunchy (that's the best part!).

MAPLE YAM BAKE WITH GRAHAM TOPPING

It's obvious that you would make this for Thanksgiving dinner, but I don't want you to go all year without making it just for that reason. I definitely don't! I've been known to make this on occasion for my family's traditional Sunday dinners, sometimes served next to a great roast beef. I think it adds so much warmth and comfort to our time around the table. Besides, who doesn't like to sit down to an unexpected piece of Thanksgiving?

Serves 6 to 8

2 (40-ounce) cans yams, drained

¾ cup maple syrup

5 tablespoons butter, melted, divided

2 eggs

¼ cup milk

1 teaspoon vanilla extract

½ teaspoon salt

1 cup coarsely crushed graham crackers

■ Preheat oven to 375 degrees F. Coat a 3-quart casserole dish with cooking spray.

■ In a large bowl, with a potato masher or electric mixer, mash yams well. Add the maple syrup, 4 tablespoons butter, the eggs, milk, vanilla, and salt; mix well. Spoon into prepared casserole dish.

■ In a small bowl, combine graham crackers and remaining 1 tablespoon butter. Sprinkle evenly over potato mixture.

■ Bake 35 to 40 minutes, or until the center is set and the topping is golden.

BEST-EVER
BROCCOLI STUFFING BAKE

As far as crowd-pleasing casseroles go, this is one of the best ever. I've even seen kids ask for seconds...of a casserole that's loaded with broccoli! It must be something about it being combined with flavorful stuffing mix and lots of cheesy, creamy goodness. Whatever it is, it's usually one of the first dishes to disappear from the spread.

Serves 6 to 8

1 cup mayonnaise

1 (10-¾-ounce) can cream of celery soup

½ cup chopped onion

¼ teaspoon black pepper

2 (10-ounce) packages frozen chopped broccoli, thawed

1 cup shredded sharp cheddar cheese

1 (6-ounce) box herbed stuffing mix

½ stick butter, melted

- Preheat oven to 350 degrees F. Coat a 3-quart casserole dish with cooking spray.

- In a medium bowl, combine mayonnaise, soup, onion, and pepper; mix well.

- Place half the broccoli in the casserole dish. Sprinkle with half the cheese and half the stuffing mix. Pour half the butter and half the soup mixture over stuffing. Repeat layers one more time.

- Bake 35 to 40 minutes, or until hot in center.

MEDITERRANEAN SPAGHETTI SQUASH

Spaghetti squash is such a cool vegetable. I mean, how many vegetables do you know that can trick you into thinking you're eating something else? When you scrape the insides of the spaghetti squash, it actually pulls apart in noodle-like strands, making it a healthy substitute for pasta. A lot of people like to serve this with a simple spaghetti sauce, but I prefer to top mine with fresh-tasting Mediterranean ingredients.

Serves 4 to 6

1 spaghetti squash

2 tablespoons olive oil

1 onion, chopped

2 cloves garlic, minced

3 plum tomatoes, chopped

¾ cup crumbled feta cheese

3 tablespoons sliced black olives

2 tablespoons chopped fresh basil

- Place about 1 inch of water in a soup pot; place the whole squash in the pot. Bring to a boil over medium-high heat, cover, and cook 25 to 30 minutes, or until tender.

- When squash is tender, remove it to a cutting board and allow to cool slightly, about 15 minutes. Cut squash in half lengthwise, then use a spoon to remove and discard seeds. Scrape the inside of squash with a fork, shredding it into noodle-like strands. Place in a medium bowl.

- Meanwhile, in a large skillet over medium heat, heat oil until hot, but not smoking. Cook onion until tender, stirring occasionally. Add garlic; cook 2 to 3 minutes or until it begins to turn golden, stirring occasionally. Add tomatoes and cook until warmed through, stirring occasionally.

- Add tomato mixture, feta cheese, olives, and basil to spaghetti squash and toss. Serve warm.

Did you know that 1 cup of cooked spaghetti has about 220 calories, and 42 grams of carbs, compared to the same amount of cooked spaghetti squash, which has only 42 calories and 10 grams of carbs? That's why I like to mix this into my weeknight dinner routine. MCM

BAKED CAULIFLOWER NUGGETS

I'm not really one to watch my carbs (it's kind of hard to do when you're a foodie like me!), but I do like to make lighter substitutions from time to time. So, when I need a break from French fries and potato tots, I bake up these crunchy and cheesy cauliflower nuggets. They pair great with pretty much anything you've got on your plate and make for a great snack too.

Makes about 24

6 cups water

5 cups cauliflower florets (about 1-¼ to 1-½ heads cauliflower)

¾ cup shredded pepper jack cheese

⅓ cup grated Parmesan cheese

½ cup plain bread crumbs

¼ cup finely chopped onion

1 egg, beaten

1 teaspoon garlic powder

½ teaspoon salt

¼ teaspoon black pepper

■ Preheat oven to 400 degrees F. Coat 2 baking sheets with cooking spray.

■ In a large saucepan over high heat, bring water to a boil; cook cauliflower 10 minutes, or until fork-tender. If you're in a time crunch, you could use frozen cauliflower that's been thawed (there's no difference and there's no boiling required!). Drain well and place cauliflower in a food processor. Pulse 10 to 15 seconds, or until cauliflower is coarsely chopped.

■ In a large bowl, combine cauliflower and remaining ingredients; mix well. With a soup spoon, form about a tablespoon of cauliflower mixture into a nugget shape and place on baking sheet. Repeat until all mixture is used up.

■ Bake 15 minutes, or until the bottoms are golden. Turn them over and bake about 10 more minutes, or until both sides are golden brown. Serve warm.

Rather than drag out my big food processor, I often use my mini hand chopper to chop the cauliflower. I do it in a few batches and done. It doesn't get any easier than that!

MCM

SWEET AND SMOKY BAKED BEANS

I know it may not be traditional, but you can save yourself hours of time by starting out with a can of baked beans. And the best part is, no one will be able to tell the difference. When they're done, they taste just as special as if they were slow-cooked. The French-fried onions and bacon bits give it a nice crunch too!

Serves 6 to 7

2 (16-ounce) cans
baked beans

1 (6-ounce) package
French-fried
onions, divided

¼ cup molasses

¼ cup real bacon bits

2 tablespoons
Dijon mustard

1 tablespoon butter,
softened

■ Preheat oven to 350 degrees F. Coat a 2-quart casserole dish with cooking spray.

■ In a medium bowl, combine all ingredients, except ½ package French-fried onions; mix well then pour into baking dish. Top with remaining French-fried onions.

■ Bake 25 to 30 minutes, or until bubbly and onions are crispy. Serve piping hot.

AP-PEEL-ING RED CABBAGE

So many of my favorite fall comfort foods are in the same color palette; there's lots of brown and orange. So, to add some visual appeal, I like to include this vibrant red cabbage in my dinner spread. And, aside from looking good, it fills my house with the most amazing smells while it cooks up in the slow cooker. How can you go wrong with a side dish like this?

Serves 8 to 10

1 red cabbage, shredded (about 2-¾ pounds)

2 tart apples, peeled and sliced

½ stick butter

¼ cup apple cider vinegar

1 bay leaf

¼ cup brown sugar

1 teaspoon salt

¼ teaspoon black pepper

¼ teaspoon ground cloves

■ In a 5- to 6-quart slow cooker, combine all ingredients; toss gently to coat.

■ Cover and cook on LOW 3-½ hours, or until liquid is absorbed and cabbage is tender. Discard bay leaf. Serve hot or cold.

You can use any type of vinegar in this recipe, everything from balsamic to rice wine vinegar. I like to use apple cider vinegar since it adds a sweet touch and helps bring all the flavors together. Whatever you do, don't skip out on the vinegar, since the acid is what helps the cabbage retain its vibrant color while it cooks. MCM

HONEY-GLAZED BRUSSELS SPROUTS

This is the recipe that's going to help you convince the non-believers that Brussels sprouts are delicious (even David on QVC)! I've found that roasting them gives them a great texture and enhances their flavor. And if the roasting still isn't enough for the Brussels sprouts-haters in your life, then the honey-balsamic glaze will definitely do the trick!

Serves 5 to 6

2 tablespoons olive oil

1 teaspoon salt

¼ teaspoon black pepper

1-½ pounds Brussels sprouts, trimmed and cut in half

2 tablespoons balsamic vinegar

2 teaspoons honey

- ■ Preheat oven to 400 degrees F. Line a baking sheet with foil and coat with cooking spray.

- ■ In a large bowl, combine oil, salt, and pepper; add Brussels sprouts and toss until evenly coated. Place on baking sheet.

- ■ Bake 20 to 25 minutes, or until tender and the edges begin to brown.

- ■ Meanwhile, in a small saucepan over low heat, combine vinegar and honey. Heat 8 to 10 minutes, or until mixture has thickened slightly. Toss with Brussels sprouts and serve. You can pop them back in the oven for a few more minutes, if you'd like, to get the sugars in the honey to caramelize.

Still haven't tried Brussels sprouts? Some people say they taste like cabbage, while others say they've got more of a broccoli flavor. I can see where both sides are coming from, but I really think they've got a flavor of their own. You're just going to have to try it to see where you stand. MCM

SUPER-STUFFED PIZZA ZUCCHINI BOATS

All aboard the S.S. Pizza Boats! You'll want to "sail" these right into your mouth because they're stuffed full of pizza flavors. My version includes fresh tomatoes and basil, to give these pizza boats a lighter taste. I also like to include red pepper flakes into my seasoning to add a little kick. Whether or not you choose to include the sausage or another pizza topping is up to you. I'm all about choices!

Makes 4

2 medium zucchini

2 cloves garlic, minced

1 tomato, seeded and finely chopped

½ cup cooked, crumbled Italian sausage

1 teaspoon Italian seasoning

¼ teaspoon crushed red pepper flakes

2 tablespoons olive oil

¾ cup (3 ounces) shredded Parmesan cheese, divided

2 teaspoons fresh basil, chopped

■ Preheat oven to 400 degrees F. Coat a 9- x 13-inch baking dish with cooking spray.

■ Cut zucchini in half lengthwise; scoop out pulp and seeds, leaving ¼-inch shell (use a small spoon for this). Reserve pulp from both zucchini and chop.

■ In a medium bowl, combine the pulp from the zucchini, garlic, tomato, sausage, Italian seasoning, red pepper flakes, olive oil, and ½ cup cheese. Spoon mixture evenly into the zucchini shells. Place stuffed zucchini in prepared baking dish; cover with foil.

■ Bake 25 minutes, or until zucchini are tender. Sprinkle with remaining cheese. Bake uncovered 5 minutes more, or until cheese is melted. Top with fresh basil and serve.

PEAS 'N' CARROTS ORZO SKILLET

It may look like rice, but it's not—orzo is actually little pasta! It's easy to get bored of having the same side dishes all the time, so this is a good one for changing things up. I also like to make it in the springtime when everyone (including me!) is craving fresh and bright flavors. What I've discovered is that people really like to eat their peas and carrots this way.

Serves 4 to 6

8 ounces orzo pasta

½ stick butter

¼ cup diced onion

1-½ cups frozen peas and carrots, thawed

½ teaspoon garlic powder

½ teaspoon salt

¼ teaspoon black pepper

2 tablespoons chopped fresh basil

1 tablespoon lemon juice

- ■ Cook pasta according to package directions. Drain and rinse.

- ■ In a large skillet over medium-high heat, melt butter; cook onion 3 to 4 minutes, or until tender.

- ■ Add pasta, peas and carrots, garlic powder, salt, and pepper; mix well. Cook 3 to 5 minutes or until heated through, stirring occasionally. Stir in basil and lemon juice and serve.

I like to let this heat up for a bit longer in the skillet as it allows the orzo to begin to crisp up, almost to the point of getting a real nutty flavor. MCM

AMISH PICKLED RELISH

Some of the largest Amish communities in the country are close to where I live in Philly, which means that it's easy to find a place with great Pennsylvania Dutch-style food. One dish that I particularly enjoy is what the Amish call "chowchow." It's a simple pickled relish that's made with lots of veggies and beans. Serve it up at your next potluck as a great alternative to potato salad or coleslaw, and watch everyone dig in.

Serves 8 to 10

2 cups water

1 cup apple cider vinegar

2-1/2 cups sugar

1/2 teaspoon celery seed

1/2 teaspoon salt

1 (14-1/2-ounce) can sliced carrots, drained

1 (14-1/2-ounce) can cut green beans, drained

1 (14-1/2-ounce) can cut yellow wax beans, drained

1 (7.75-ounce) can garbanzo beans, rinsed and drained

1 (15-ounce) can red kidney beans, rinsed and drained

1 onion, cut into 1/2-inch pieces

1 red bell pepper, cut into 1/2-inch pieces

■ In a medium saucepan over high heat, bring water, vinegar, sugar, celery seed, and salt to a boil, stirring occasionally.

■ Meanwhile, in a large bowl, combine remaining ingredients.

■ Pour vinegar mixture over vegetables and toss until evenly coated. Let cool, cover and refrigerate until chilled. (This can be stored in the refrigerator for weeks and is the perfect side dish for any meal.)

Opening cans used to be such a hassle, but now that I found the best can opener ever, it's such a breeze. Yup, just in case you're wondering, it's the one you've seen me use on QVC! MCM

Life is too short to skip out on dessert! I'm not afraid to be caught dunking my oversized cookies in a glass of milk or digging my fork into a great big slice of pie. If anything, having a sweet tooth makes me even sweeter! MCM

DESSERTS

ALL-AMERICAN BLUEBERRY PIE

I may be a little bit biased when I say that blueberry pie is the ultimate all-American dessert, because it's MY favorite. There's nothing more welcoming than a blueberry pie. The part I like best is digging my fork into the pie and having the blueberries ooze out and onto my plate. That's how you know you've got the real deal. Oh, and don't forget to serve it with a scoop of ice cream!

Serves 6 to 8

¾ cup sugar

⅓ cup all-purpose flour

½ teaspoon ground cinnamon

2 pints fresh blueberries

1 tablespoon lemon juice

1 tablespoon butter, cut into small pieces

1 (14.1-ounce) package refrigerated rolled pie crusts

1 egg, beaten

If the idea of making a lattice pie crust freaks you out, no worries. You can always place the top pie crust on, pinch the edges, and cut a few slits in the top dough to allow the steam to escape during baking. MCM

■ Preheat oven to 400 degrees F.

■ In a large bowl, combine sugar, flour, and cinnamon; mix well. Add blueberries, lemon juice, and butter and toss until blueberries are evenly coated. Unroll 1 pie crust and place in a 9-inch deep dish pie plate. Spoon blueberry mixture into crust.

■ Unroll remaining pie crust and, using a knife, cut into 10 (¾-inch) wide strips. To create a lattice top, lay five strips, evenly spaced, across filling. Fold every other strip back half way. Take one of the remaining five strips and lay it across the pie in the opposite direction; unfold the folded strips over this one. Now, fold back the strips that lie beneath this strip and lay your second strip across. Continue doing this weave pattern, folding back every other strip each time you add a cross strip. Trim ends of lattice strips, press together with bottom pie crust and flute. Brush with beaten egg.

■ Bake 45 to 50 minutes, or until golden brown and juice has begun to bubble. Place on a wire rack to cool. Serve at room temp or refrigerated. It cuts so much better when it's been chilled.

HEAD-TURNING CHOCOLATE CREAM PIE

Set this pie out somewhere in plain sight and get ready to turn some heads. I've found that no one can take their eyes off of this decadent-looking dessert. From the silky chocolate pudding to the fluffy and homemade whipped topping, this pie deserves to be center stage.

Serves 6 to 8

1 refrigerated rolled pie crust (from a 14.1-ounce package)

⅔ cup granulated sugar

¼ cup cocoa powder

3 tablespoons cornstarch

¼ teaspoon salt

2 cups cold milk

¼ cup chocolate syrup

1 teaspoon vanilla extract

1 cup heavy cream

2 tablespoons powdered sugar

Shaved chocolate or sprinkles for garnish

■ Unroll pie crust and place in a 9-inch deep dish pie plate, pressing crust firmly into pie plate; prick the bottom several times with a fork and flute edges, if desired. (Pricking the dough prevents the crust from bubbling up when baking.) Bake pie crust according to package directions; let cool.

■ In a medium saucepan, combine granulated sugar, cocoa, cornstarch, and salt. Gradually stir in milk and chocolate syrup. Bring to a boil over medium heat, stirring constantly. Remove from heat and stir in vanilla. Pour into pie crust, then chill 1 hour.

■ Meanwhile, in a medium bowl, with an electric mixer on medium-low speed, beat heavy cream and powdered sugar until stiff peaks form. Spread whipped cream evenly over pie, cover loosely, and chill 8 hours or overnight. When ready to serve, garnish with shaved chocolate, if desired.

PERFECTLY PUMPKIN CHEESECAKE PIE

I've made some pretty tough choices at the Thanksgiving table, especially when it comes to dessert. After feasting on just about everything, it's hard to pick just one dessert to make room for. There's cheesecake, there's pie, and sometimes even a cake. So, I decided to make things a little easier by combining two of my favorites in one. There's always room for a slice of this creamy pumpkin cheesecake pie (and maybe you can still have a piece of cake, too.)

Serves 8 to 10

1 prepared 10-inch graham cracker pie crust

1 egg yolk, beaten

2 whole eggs

2 (8-ounce) packages cream cheese, softened

¾ cup sugar

1 (15-ounce) can pure pumpkin (not pumpkin pie filling)

1-½ teaspoons ground cinnamon

½ teaspoon ground ginger

■ Preheat oven to 350 degrees F. Brush pie crust with egg yolk and bake for 5 minutes; set aside. (Baking it will seal the crust and prevent it from getting soggy.)

■ In a large bowl with an electric mixer, beat the 2 whole eggs, cream cheese, and sugar until smooth. Add pumpkin, cinnamon, and ginger and continue beating until well blended. Spoon mixture into pie crust.

■ Bake 40 to 45 minutes, or until the center is set. Let cool at room temperature, then refrigerate 3 hours or overnight.

As if this weren't rich enough, I often like to dollop each slice with a homemade maple whipped cream. To make it, all you have to do is whip 1 cup of heavy cream with an electric mixer for 3 to 4 minutes, or until soft peaks form. Then, drizzle in 2 tablespoons of real maple syrup and 2 tablespoons of powdered sugar and continue whipping until stiff peaks form. Keep it refrigerated until you're ready to serve. MCM

MINI APPLE PIE POCKETS

I've always liked what I call "pocket foods." What I mean by that is food that's sort of contained inside something—like a meat pie or a calzone. Most of the pocket foods I eat are savory, so this one of fun to come up with. It's a great dessert that you can just grab with your hands and eat wherever and whenever. It doesn't get better than that.

Makes 16

2 tablespoons butter

2 large green apples, peeled, cored, and cut into ½-inch chunks

¼ cup plus 1 tablespoon granulated sugar, divided

2 tablespoons brown sugar

1-½ teaspoons ground cinnamon

1 (14.1-ounce) package refrigerated rolled pie crusts

1 egg, beaten

1 tablespoon milk

■ Preheat oven to 400 degrees F. Line 2 baking sheets with parchment paper.

■ In a large skillet over medium heat, melt butter. Stir in apples, ¼ cup granulated sugar, the brown sugar, and cinnamon. Cook 5 to 7 minutes, or until apples are softened, stirring occasionally; set aside.

■ Unroll both pie crusts and using a 3-inch cookie cutter or drinking glass, cut out circles. Place a teaspoon of apple mixture into center of each circle.

■ In a small bowl, mix egg and milk. Brush egg mixture around edge of each circle; fold dough over fruit and pinch edges together. Brush top of each pie with remaining egg mixture and sprinkle with remaining 1 tablespoon granulated sugar. Place on prepared baking sheets.

■ Bake 12 to 15 minutes, or until pies are golden brown. Serve warm.

If you would like to make your own homemade pie crust, just combine 4 cups all-purpose flour, 1-¾ cups shortening, 3 tablespoons sugar, and 2 tablespoons salt in a bowl. Now, with a pastry cutter or two forks "cut" the shortening with the flour until it's crumbly. Add 1 egg mixed together with a ½ cup of ice cold water to the flour mixture. Stir until the dough comes together. Divide the dough into 4 equal-sized pieces. Each piece is enough for one pie crust. Keep the dough refrigerated until ready to use. MCM

STRAWBERRY RHUBARB COOKIE COBBLER

Traditionally, this ruby red cobbler is topped with buttermilk biscuits or a biscuit-like crust, but I'm not really a traditional guy—I'm a guy who likes cookies. That's why my topping is made with sugar cookie dough! I found that it's a tasty way to add a little more sweetness to a tart dessert.

Serves 6 to 8

1 (16-ounce) container fresh strawberries

1 (16-ounce) package frozen rhubarb, thawed

1 cup sugar

2 tablespoons butter, softened

1 tablespoon cornstarch

1 teaspoon vanilla extract

1 (16.25-ounce) package refrigerated sugar cookie dough

■ Preheat oven to 400 degrees F. Coat an 8-inch square baking dish with cooking spray.

■ In a large bowl, combine strawberries, rhubarb, sugar, butter, cornstarch, and vanilla; mix well then pour into prepared baking dish.

■ Cut cookie dough into ¼-inch slices and place them on top of the strawberry mixture, covering it.

■ Bake 40 to 45 minutes, or until the filling is bubbling hot and cookie topping is golden. Serve warm (with a big scoop of vanilla ice cream!).

If fresh strawberries are available, by all means use them! If not, frozen ones will work just fine. Be sure to thaw them first. MCM

SLOW COOKER APPLE COBBLER

I like to serve this when I have company coming over for dinner. I get everything into my slow cooker and turn it on as soon as they walk in. That way, as we have drinks and dinner, the whole house is filled with the rich scent of cinnamon and apples. And by dessert time, everyone is ready to dig in and enjoy the goodness.

Serves 6 to 8

8 tart apples, peeled, cored, and cut into ½-inch slices

¼ cup granulated sugar

2 tablespoons plus ¼ cup all-purpose flour, divided

2 tablespoons butter, melted

1 teaspoon ground cinnamon

¾ cup quick-cooking oatmeal

¼ cup light brown sugar

½ stick butter, cut into small pieces

- ■ Coat a 4- to 5-quart slow cooker with cooking spray.

- ■ In a large bowl, toss apples, granulated sugar, 2 tablespoons flour, the melted butter, and cinnamon. Place mixture in slow cooker.

- ■ In a medium bowl, combine oatmeal, brown sugar, the remaining ¼ cup flour, and the butter pieces; mix until crumbly. Sprinkle over apples.

- ■ Cover and cook on LOW for 3 hours, or until apples are tender and topping is golden.

LEMON POPPY SEED POUND CAKE

This dessert is a real classic. It's bright and happy and bursting with citrusy flavor, which makes it the ideal dessert for serving at a weekend brunch. Just thinking about the next time I'm going to make this for my family makes me smile. I have a feeling it'll do the same for you, too.

Serves 10 to 12

3 cups all-purpose flour, plus extra for dusting

2 sticks butter, softened

2-½ cups granulated sugar

5 eggs

2 teaspoons lemon extract

1 teaspoon baking powder

¼ teaspoon salt

1 cup milk

2 tablespoons poppy seeds

Zest of 1 lemon

GLAZE

1-½ cups powdered sugar

2 tablespoons lemon juice

■ Preheat oven to 350 degrees F. Coat a 12-cup Bundt pan with cooking spray and lightly dust with flour.

■ In a large bowl with an electric mixer, beat butter and sugar until fluffy. Add eggs and lemon extract and mix until creamy.

■ In a medium bowl, combine 3 cups flour, the baking powder, and salt; mix well. Gradually beat flour mixture into lemon mixture alternating it with milk, until batter is smooth. Stir in poppy seeds and lemon zest. Pour batter into prepared pan.

■ Bake 65 to 70 minutes, or until a toothpick inserted in cake comes out clean. Let cool 20 minutes, then invert onto a wire rack to cool completely.

■ To make glaze, in a medium bowl, whisk powdered sugar and lemon juice until smooth. Drizzle over cake.

FORGOT-THE-MILK CHOCOLATE CAKE

How many times have you run out to the store to buy ingredients for a recipe and realized that you forgot to get something once you're already home? (This is why lists are important!) Well, that's sort of what happened to me the day I planned on baking a chocolate cake and forgot to get the milk. Luckily, after a little experimenting I came up with a moist and chocolaty cake that doesn't need it. You're going to love this one.

Serves 12 to 15

3 cups all-purpose flour

⅓ cup cocoa powder

1-¾ cups sugar

2 teaspoons baking soda

½ teaspoon salt

2 teaspoons white vinegar

2 teaspoons vanilla extract

⅔ cup vegetable oil

1-¾ cups water

Dark Chocolate
Buttercream Frosting
(see note)

■ Preheat oven to 350 degrees F. Coat a 9- x 13-inch baking dish with cooking spray.

■ In a large bowl with an electric mixer, beat flour, cocoa powder, sugar, baking soda, and salt; mix well. Add remaining ingredients, except frosting, and beat until batter is smooth; pour into prepared baking dish.

■ Bake 30 to 35 minutes, or until a toothpick inserted in center comes out clean; let cool. Frost with my Dark Chocolate Buttercream.

To make my Dark Chocolate Buttercream Frosting, all you need to do is beat 4 cups powdered sugar, 1 stick softened butter, 1/2 cup half-and-half, 1 teaspoon vanilla extract, and a pinch of salt in a large bowl with an electric mixer on low for 1 to 2 minutes, or until it's smooth. Increase the speed to medium and continue beating for 1 to 2 minutes, or until creamy. Then, add 1/2 cup cocoa powder and beat a few more minutes until mixed evenly. If your frosting is too thick, add a little more half-and-half (just a very little bit at a time!). MCM

UNBEATABLE CARROT CAKE

I'm certain that no other carrot cake you've tasted before can even come close to how amazing this one is. I'm sorry if it sounds like I'm bragging, but sometimes you've just got to take pride in knowing that you've got an unbeatable recipe. This carrot cake, loaded with plenty of fresh carrot, coconut, and pecans is incredibly moist and flavorful. Bake it up and share with the neighbors—it's bound to make them smile.

Serves 10 to 12

2 cups all-purpose flour, plus extra for dusting

2 cups sugar

1-½ cups vegetable oil

4 eggs

2 teaspoons baking soda

2 teaspoons ground cinnamon

1 teaspoon salt

1 cup flaked coconut

3 cups grated carrots (about 1 pound)

1 cup chopped pecans

Cream Cheese Frosting (see note)

■ Preheat oven to 350 degrees F. Coat 2 (8-inch) round cake pans with cooking spray and lightly dust with flour.

■ In a large bowl with an electric mixer, combine all ingredients, except frosting, beating until a smooth batter is formed, about a minute. Make sure you do not overmix this. Pour batter evenly into prepared pans.

■ Bake 45 to 50 minutes, or until a toothpick inserted in center comes out clean. Let cool slightly, remove cakes from pans, and cool completely on wire racks.

■ Place one cake layer on a serving platter and frost top of cake. Place second layer on top of frosted layer. Frost top and sides of entire cake. Place cake in the refrigerator for at least one hour to firm up before serving.

You can frost this with a store-bought cream cheese frosting if you're short on time or, better yet, you can make your own. To make it, in a large bowl with an electric mixer, combine an 8-ounce package of softened cream cheese along with 2 sticks of softened butter. Add 1 teaspoon of vanilla extract and mix well. Then, gradually add in 4 cups of powdered sugar and continue to mix until smooth. MCM

HEAVEN-SENT ÉCLAIR CAKE

My head must have been in the clouds when I first came up with my version of this, since it came out looking like it was sent from the heavens (just look at that photo!). This dessert has creamy written all over it. From the creamy chocolate pudding mixture to the layer of luscious whipped topping, I don't see how anyone could resist this homemade bakery delight. I know I never can!

Serves 10 to 12

1 stick butter, cut into quarters

1 cup water

¼ teaspoon salt

1 cup all-purpose flour

4 eggs, at room temperature

3 cups milk

2 (4-serving size) packages instant chocolate pudding mix

1 (8-ounce) container frozen whipped topping, thawed

2 tablespoons chocolate syrup

■ Preheat oven to 400 degrees F. Coat a 10- x 15-inch baking sheet with cooking spray.

■ In a medium saucepan over medium-high heat, bring butter, water, and salt to a boil. Add flour all at once and stir quickly with a wooden spoon until mixture forms a ball; remove saucepan from heat. Add 1 egg to mixture and beat with a wooden spoon to blend. (Get ready to build some muscle here!) Add remaining eggs, one at a time, beating well after each egg is added. Spread mixture evenly onto prepared baking sheet. The mixture will be thick.

■ Bake 20 to 25 minutes, or until edges are golden brown. Remove from oven and let cool.

■ Meanwhile, in a large bowl with an electric mixer, beat milk and pudding mix together until thick. Spread evenly over pastry. Spread whipped topping over chocolate pudding. Refrigerate at least one hour. To add the signature chocolate topping that makes an éclair an éclair, drizzle with chocolate syrup right before serving.

PUMPKIN PATCH PINWHEELS

How much do you look forward to pumpkin season every year? If you're the person who can't wait to order pumpkin lattes at the coffee shop or who gets a double scoop of pumpkin ice cream when it's available, then I'm telling you...you've got to make this dessert now. It's a classic pumpkin dessert that never fails to impress. And since it's made with canned pumpkin, you don't even have to wait for fall to come around to enjoy it.

Serves 8 to 10

1 cup granulated sugar

¾ cup all-purpose flour

1 teaspoon baking soda

2 teaspoons pumpkin pie spice

1 cup pure pumpkin (from a 15-ounce can)

3 eggs

1 cup plus 2 tablespoons powdered sugar, divided

1 (8-ounce) package cream cheese, softened

½ stick butter

1 teaspoon vanilla extract

■ Preheat oven to 375 degrees F. Coat a rimmed 10- x 15-inch baking sheet with cooking spray.

■ In a large bowl, combine granulated sugar, flour, baking soda, and pumpkin pie spice. Stir in pumpkin and eggs. Pour mixture onto prepared baking sheet, spreading evenly. Bake 12 to 15 minutes, or until a toothpick inserted in center comes out clean.

■ Remove from oven and invert onto a clean kitchen towel that has been sprinkled with 2 tablespoons powdered sugar. While cake is still hot, roll it up in the towel jelly roll-style from the narrow end and allow to cool on a wire rack. When cool, unroll cake and remove towel.

■ Meanwhile, in a small bowl with an electric mixer on medium speed, beat cream cheese, butter, vanilla, and remaining 1 cup powdered sugar until creamy. Spread onto cake and immediately re-roll it (without towel). Place on serving platter, seam-side down and refrigerate until ready to serve. Cut into slices just before serving (they'll look just like pinwheels!).

For the final touch, sprinkle on some extra powdered sugar right before serving. MCM

CARAMEL-NUT CHEESECAKE

This cheesecake is going to blow your mind. Not only is it creamy and perfect the way a cheesecake should be, but it's got a homemade cookie crust and it's loaded with your favorite candy bars. Oh yeah, and there's a chocolate drizzle on top. (Quick, catch the drool before it lands on the page!) I'm telling you, if you can resist this dessert, then you've got some extraordinary willpower. I, on the other hand, am totally okay with saying "Yes!" to this.

Serves 12 to 14

20 chocolate sandwich cookies

½ stick butter, melted

3 (8-ounce) packages cream cheese, softened

1 cup sugar

4 eggs

1 teaspoon vanilla extract

1-½ cups coarsely chopped caramel-nut candy bars, divided (see note)

1 cup dark chocolate chips

I used Snickers® when I made this cheesecake, but to change it up you can use any other candy bar you like. MCM

■ Preheat oven to 350 degrees F.

■ Place cookies in a resealable plastic bag and, using a rolling pin or can, finely crush them. Place in a medium bowl and add butter; mix well, then pat firmly into the bottom (not the sides) of a 10-inch springform pan. Chill until ready to use.

■ In a large bowl, combine cream cheese and sugar; beat with an electric mixer on low speed until creamy. Beat in eggs, one at a time, then add vanilla; mix well. With a spoon, stir in 1 cup candy, then pour into pan.

■ Bake 55 to 60 minutes, or until firm in center; cake may crack slightly, which is totally fine. Remove from oven and let cool at room temperature. Remove the ring around the cake (there's no need to remove the bottom) and refrigerate 6 to 8 hours, or overnight to firm up.

■ Right before ready to serve, melt chocolate chips in a microwave-safe bowl 60 to 90 seconds, stirring occasionally until smooth. Place in a resealable plastic bag, cut tip off one corner of bag, and drizzle chocolate over cheesecake. Sprinkle with remaining candy. Now, it's ready to serve.

PEANUT BUTTER CUP BROWNIES

Cue the enlightening music. Turn your attention to the photo on the next page for just a moment, then come back here. Now, what's the first word that comes to mind? I hope it was "chocolate" because these are what I like to consider the "holy grail" for chocolate lovers. A homemade chocolate brownie stuffed with everyone's favorite peanut butter cups AND chocolate chips? I just hope your sweet tooth can handle it.

Makes 12 to 15

2 sticks butter, melted

¾ cup cocoa powder

2 cups sugar

4 eggs

1 cup all-purpose flour

2 teaspoons vanilla extract

½ teaspoon salt

1 (12-ounce) package semisweet chocolate chips (2 cups)

30 mini peanut butter cup candies, cut in half, divided

■ Preheat oven to 350 degrees F. Coat a 9- x 13-inch baking dish with cooking spray.

■ Place butter in a large bowl; add cocoa and stir until well blended. Add sugar; mix well. Add eggs, one at a time, mixing well after each addition. Add flour, vanilla, and salt; stir just until combined. Stir in chocolate chips and 1-⅓ cups of the peanut butter candies. Spread batter in prepared baking dish and sprinkle with remaining peanut butter candies.

■ Bake 35 to 40 minutes, or until a toothpick inserted in center comes out clean. Let cool, then cut and enjoy.

HAPPY CAMPER BROWNIES

What makes a camper happier than good weather and good friends? S'mores of course! These are perfect to bake ahead of time and take along with you no matter where you go. You don't need to gather wood, make a fire, or even find the perfect roasting stick to make these sweet treats, which is just A-OK with me, since I don't have a lot of time to go camping these days!

Makes 12 to 15

1 package brownie mix (see note)

6 graham crackers, broken into 1-inch pieces

1 (5- to 7-ounce) milk chocolate candy bar, coarsely chopped

1 cup miniature marshmallows

■ Preheat oven to 350 degrees F. Coat a 9- x 13-inch baking dish with cooking spray.

■ Prepare brownie batter according to package directions. Pour into prepared baking dish and bake only 15 minutes. (You don't want to bake these completely yet.)

■ Meanwhile, in a medium bowl, combine the graham crackers, chopped chocolate, and marshmallows, and mix well.

■ Remove par-baked brownies from oven and sprinkle chocolate and marshmallow mixture evenly over top. Bake an additional 15 to 20 minutes, or until a toothpick inserted in center comes out clean. Cool completely, then cut and enjoy.

There's a wide variety of package sizes of brownie mix. Any size will work for this recipe.

MCM

MOM-AND-POP SPICE BARS

I first tasted something similar to these bars at a great little mom-and-pop store in rural Pennsylvania, and I liked them so much I decided to come up with my own version. These made-from-scratch bars have that same great, old-fashioned taste that I think so many of us love, but with a couple of new-fashioned additions: white chocolate chips and a simple white glaze.

Makes 21 to 24

2 sticks butter, softened

2 cups firmly packed brown sugar

2 eggs

½ cup cold water

1 teaspoon baking soda

1 teaspoon ground nutmeg

1-¼ teaspoons ground cinnamon

3-½ cups all-purpose flour

1 cup raisins

1 cup white chocolate chips

1 cup powdered sugar

2 tablespoons milk

■ Preheat oven to 350 degrees F. Coat a 10- x 15-inch rimmed baking sheet with cooking spray.

■ In a large bowl with an electric mixer, cream together butter and brown sugar. Blend in eggs. On low speed, beat in water, baking soda, nutmeg, and cinnamon. Gradually mix in flour, about ⅓ at a time. Stir in raisins and chips. Spread batter on prepared baking sheet.

■ Bake 15 to 20 minutes, or until firm. Remove pan to a wire rack to cool completely, then cut into 2-inch bars.

■ In a small bowl, whisk powdered sugar and milk until smooth. Spoon glaze on each bar and allow to sit until glaze firms up.

These freeze really well, which is great since this recipe makes a whole lot of cookie bars. They take just a few minutes to thaw out before they're ready to be eaten.

MCM

OATMEAL COOKIE SANDWICHES

These take me back to my childhood, when I'd come home to a special treat after a long day at school. They're my version of a whoopie pie, and they're a real dream. Although I love taking big bites out of each one, I have to admit that my favorite part is licking off all the icing that squishes out over the edge first.

Makes 9

2 sticks butter, softened

½ cup light brown sugar

½ cup granulated sugar

2 eggs

1 teaspoon vanilla extract

1-½ cups all-purpose flour

1 teaspoon ground cinnamon

1 teaspoon baking soda

½ teaspoon salt

3 cups oats (see note)

CREAM FILLING

1-½ sticks butter, softened

2-½ cups powdered sugar

1 teaspoon vanilla extract

■ Preheat oven to 350 degrees F. Line baking sheets with parchment paper.

■ In a large bowl with an electric mixer, beat butter, brown sugar, and granulated sugar until light and fluffy. Add eggs and vanilla and mix until creamy.

■ In a medium bowl, mix flour, cinnamon, baking soda, and salt. Slowly add flour mixture into butter mixture, beating until well combined. Stir in oats; mix well. Using a medium ice cream scoop, drop about 2 tablespoons dough onto prepared baking sheet, making 18 cookies. Bake 12 to 15 minutes, or until golden brown. Remove to wire racks to cool completely.

■ Meanwhile, to make filling, in a large bowl with an electric mixer, beat the butter for 2 minutes or until light and fluffy. Slowly add powdered sugar and vanilla; beating until smooth. Spread filling evenly on flat side of half of the cookies. Place remaining cookies flat side down on the filling, pressing down lightly until the filling starts to ooze out. Store in an airtight container in the refrigerator.

I've tried this with both quick-cooking and old-fashioned oatmeal and both worked well, so no matter what you have on hand you should be good to go. MCM

SOFT 'N' CRISPY CHOCOLATE CHIP COOKIES

First you have one, then another, and another...and before you know it the cookie jar is empty! (At least that's been my experience with these.) The oats and the crispy rice cereal add seriously good texture to these cookies. And since my recipe makes plenty, you'll have enough to share (that's if you want to...).

Makes 3-½ dozen

½ cup old-fashioned oats

2-¼ cups all-purpose flour

1-½ teaspoons baking soda

1 teaspoon salt

2 sticks butter, softened

¾ cup firmly packed brown sugar

¾ cup granulated sugar

1-½ teaspoons vanilla extract

2 eggs

1 (12-ounce) package semisweet chocolate chips (2 cups)

1-½ cups crispy rice cereal

■ Preheat oven to 350 degrees F. In a food processor or blender, pulse oats until fine.

■ In a large bowl, combine flour, oats, baking soda, and salt. In another large bowl, with an electric mixer, cream together butter, brown sugar, granulated sugar, and vanilla. Add eggs and beat until smooth. Stir in oats mixture; mix well. Stir chocolate chips and cereal into dough; mix well.

■ Drop rounded teaspoonfuls onto ungreased baking sheets, about 2 inches apart.

■ Bake 10 to 14 minutes, or until cookies are golden. Cool 5 minutes, then remove to a wire rack to cool completely. Enjoy.

WALNUT CRESCENT COOKIES

These nutty cookies are great on a holiday cookie platter. The powdered sugar makes them look like they've been dusted with snow and the crescent shape gives them a simple decorative look. Make these cookies with your family or a group of friends and create some tasty memories. Don't forget to turn on the holiday music!

Makes 3 dozen

2 sticks butter

1-¼ cups powdered sugar, divided

2 teaspoons vanilla extract

1 teaspoon water

2 cups all-purpose flour

1-½ cups chopped walnuts

- Preheat oven to 350 degrees F.

- In a large bowl with an electric mixer, cream butter and ¼ cup sugar. Add vanilla and water; mix well. Gradually add flour and continue to mix until well combined. (The dough will be a little stiff.) Add walnuts and mix well. Using about 1 tablespoon of dough per cookie, form each cookie into a log and bend to form a crescent-shape; place on ungreased baking sheets.

- Bake 18 to 20 minutes, or until set.

- Place remaining sugar in a shallow dish. Remove cookies from oven and, when cool enough to handle, roll in powdered sugar. Be gentle as they will be fragile.

CRÈME BRÛLÉE RICE PUDDING

Here's your chance to take a "crack" at something you already love with a tasty new twist. I combined a comforting American classic (rice pudding) with a dessert that many of us consider fancy (crème brûlée). It's surprisingly easy to do and the results are so decadent it's hard to ignore the cravings!

Serves 4

2 cups cooked rice

3 cups half-and-half

⅓ cup plus ¾ cup sugar, divided

A pinch of salt

1 tablespoon butter

1 teaspoon vanilla extract

■ In a large saucepan over medium heat, combine rice, half-and-half, ⅓ cup sugar, the salt, and butter. Cook about 20 minutes or until thickened, stirring often. Add vanilla and stir.

■ Pour into 4 (1 cup) ramekins and chill at least 2 hours, or overnight.

■ Shortly before serving, in a small skillet over medium heat, melt remaining ¾ cup sugar until it's liquidy and golden. Carefully top each ramekin of rice pudding with the melted sugar. Chill an additional 15 to 20 minutes, or until sugar has hardened and you've got a golden layer of goodness on top. Serve immediately, or keep refrigerated until ready to serve.

CROISSANT BREAD PUDDING

This may very well be the most decadent dessert in my whole book, but that's okay, because this is the kind of dessert you make when you need to pull out all the stops. It's a dessert that shouts, "Hello! I'm here and I'm ready to rock your world!" So, set aside the white bread for another day, buy yourself some croissants, and get ready to bake up the most fabulous bread pudding you've ever tasted.

Serves 6 to 8

1-½ cups heavy cream

½ cup granulated sugar

¼ teaspoon ground cinnamon

4 egg yolks

6 croissants, (dinner size, not minis) torn into small pieces

½ cup white baking chips

½ cup raisins

½ cup light brown sugar

■ Preheat oven to 300 degrees F. Coat a 2-quart casserole dish with cooking spray.

■ In a large bowl, combine heavy cream, granulated sugar, cinnamon, and egg yolks; mix well. Add torn croissants, white baking chips, and raisins to cream mixture; stir until thoroughly combined. Spoon mixture into prepared casserole dish.

■ Bake 45 to 50 minutes, or until center is set. Sprinkle with brown sugar and continue baking until sugar is melted, about 5 minutes. Serve warm.

Since I only make this for special occasions, I don't feel guilty serving something this decadent. And when I do, I like to top each serving with some lightly whipped cream. All you have to do is, in a medium bowl with an electric mixer, beat 1 cup heavy cream for 1 minute. Add 1 tablespoon sugar and 1 tablespoon vanilla; continue beating 3 to 4 more minutes, or until stiff peaks form. MCM

BEST-EVER TIRAMISU

Hands down, my favorite Italian dessert has to be tiramisù. I don't know if it has to do with being a big coffee drinker or because it's made with lots of creamy mascarpone cheese, but honestly, I don't think too much about it. All I know is that this dessert is close to my heart. It's a classic that's I always welcome with an open mouth!

Serves 6 to 9

1 cup warm water

1 tablespoon instant coffee granules

½ teaspoon vanilla extract

16 ounces mascarpone cheese

1 cup sugar

2 cups (1 pint) heavy cream

2 (3-ounce) packages ladyfingers (see note)

½ teaspoon cocoa powder

■ In a small bowl, combine water, coffee granules, and vanilla; stir to dissolve the coffee, then set aside.

■ In a large bowl with an electric mixer, beat mascarpone cheese and sugar until smooth; set aside. (Psst! Now would be a good time to sneak a fingerful!)

■ In a medium bowl with an electric mixer on medium-high speed, beat heavy cream until stiff peaks form. Fold 1-½ cups of whipped cream into mascarpone cheese mixture until well combined.

■ Line the bottom of an 8-inch square baking dish with ladyfingers, slightly overlapping to fit. Drizzle half the coffee mixture evenly over ladyfingers. Spoon half the cheese mixture over the ladyfingers. Top with more ladyfingers and repeat with coffee mixture and cheese mixture. (If you find yourself with extra ladyfingers, consider yourself lucky... you now have something to snack on later.)

■ Spoon remaining whipped cream over the top and sprinkle with cocoa. Cover and chill at least 4 hours before serving.

MINT CHOCOLATE CHIP ICE CREAM SANDWICHES

All the best ice cream cakes have one thing in common: the "crunchies." That's the layer of cookie bits that usually make up the cake's crust or are sandwiched in between layers of ice cream. I love the crunchies so much I thought I'd turn the ice cream cake on its head and came up with these sandwiches, which feature lots of crunchy goodness. Of course, I used my favorite ice cream to make them, too.

Makes 9 to 18

1 (14.3-ounce) package chocolate sandwich cookies

⅓ cup butter, melted

1 quart mint chocolate chip ice cream, slightly softened

■ Place cookies in a gallon-sized resealable plastic bag. Using a rolling pin or can, crush the cookies until they're finely crushed. In a medium bowl, combine cookie crumbs with butter; mix well.

■ Line an 8-inch square baking dish with aluminum foil, letting some of the extra foil hang over the edges, so you can grab onto it later. Press half the cookie mixture firmly into the bottom of prepared baking dish. Spread the ice cream over the crust, then press remaining cookie mixture gently over ice cream. Cover and freeze at least 6 hours.

■ When frozen solid, remove the ice cream sandwich by lifting the foil. Discard the foil, and cut into 9 squares, then cut each square in half diagonally. These are a nice size, so you can serve just one triangle per person or, if they deserve a little more, a whole square. Keep them frozen until you're ready to serve.

If the mint chocolate chip ice cream you bought doesn't have a lot of chocolate chips in it, stir a cup or so of chocolate chips into the softened ice cream before assembling the layers. I also like to wrap these individually in plastic wrap, so that they're easy to grab from the freezer. MCM

FUDGY CUPCAKES WITH CHOCOLATE GANACHE

Cupcakes make people happy, and everyone who knows me (from my close family to my extended QVC family) knows that I like making people happy. That's why I came up with a cupcake that always makes people smile. Inside each one of these ganache-topped, vanilla delights is a fudgy chocolate filling that's just waiting to be discovered. I bet you're smiling just thinking about them.

Makes 24

1 (8-ounce) package cream cheese, softened

⅓ cup sugar

1 egg

1 cup (6 ounces) semi-sweet chocolate chips, divided

1 (16.5-ounce) package yellow cake mix, batter prepared according to package directions

GANACHE FROSTING

1 cup (6 ounces) semi-sweet chocolate chips

¾ cup heavy cream

- ■ Preheat oven to 350 degrees F. Line 24 muffin cups with paper liners.

- ■ In a large bowl with an electric mixer, beat cream cheese, sugar, and egg until creamy.

- ■ Place ¼ cup chocolate chips in a microwave-safe bowl and microwave about 30 seconds, or until melted; stir until smooth. Beat melted chocolate into cream cheese mixture. With a spoon, stir in remaining chocolate chips; set aside.

- ■ Fill each muffin cup two-thirds full with cake batter. Drop a heaping teaspoon of cream cheese mixture in center of batter in each cup.

- ■ Bake 15 to 20 minutes, or until a toothpick inserted in cake part comes out clean. Allow to cool completely.

- ■ To make the to-die-for frosting, place 1 cup chocolate chips in a bowl. In a small saucepan over medium heat, bring heavy cream to a boil, stirring constantly. Pour over chocolate chips and stir until smooth. Let cool 5 to 10 minutes, or until slightly thickened. Spoon over the top of each cupcake. Refrigerate until ready to serve.

KEY LIME PIE SHORTBREAD BARS

Your grandma may be famous for baking up the best lemon cookie bars, but I'm willing to bet you can steal some of that fame by baking up an upgraded version of her classic recipe. These cookie bars feature a thick layer of key lime pie-flavored filling over a crumbly shortbread cookie crust. Every bite tastes like paradise.

Makes 12 to 16

1-½ cups finely crushed shortbread cookies (see note)

3 tablespoons butter, melted

1 (8-ounce) package cream cheese, softened

1 (14-ounce) can sweetened condensed milk

¼ cup key lime juice

1 tablespoon lime zest

- Preheat oven to 350 degrees F. Coat an 8-inch square baking dish with cooking spray.

- In a small bowl, use a fork to thoroughly combine cookie crumbs and butter. Press evenly into bottom of prepared baking dish.

- In a medium bowl with an electric mixer, beat cream cheese until light and fluffy. Gradually beat in condensed milk until smooth. Beat in lime juice and zest. Spread over crust.

- Bake about 35 minutes, or until center is set. Cool 30 minutes, then chill at least 3 hours before cutting into bars and serving.

You can absolutely make these with other kinds of cookies, if you're not a big fan of shortbread. I've tried them with graham crackers and coconut cookies, and both make a great combo with the key lime flavor. MCM

SALTY CARAMEL BREAK-UP

Here's a quick and easy treat that you can make anytime and keep in the pantry for when those cravings kick in. Sweet and salty, this homemade candy has all the bases covered. It's also good for welcoming new neighbors to the neighborhood or gifting to friends on special occasions. Everyone loves it!

Makes about 1-½ pounds

3 cups thin pretzels sticks, broken into 1-inch pieces

2 sticks butter

1 cup light brown sugar

1 (12-ounce) package semisweet chocolate chips (2 cups)

- Preheat oven to 375 degrees F. Line a 10- x 15-inch rimmed baking sheet with parchment paper. Spread pretzel pieces on top, then set aside.

- In a small saucepan over medium heat, combine butter and brown sugar and bring to a boil. Cook 3 minutes without stirring, then carefully pour over pretzels. (Mixture will be very hot.)

- Bake 5 minutes, then place baking sheet on wire rack and sprinkle chocolate chips evenly over the top. When chocolate chips are softened, use a spatula to spread them evenly over the caramel layer.

- Let cool 2 to 3 hours, or until hard. Break into pieces. Store at room temperature.

NOTES

NOTES

NOTES

RECIPES IN ALPHABETICAL ORDER

RECIPES IN ALPHABETICAL ORDER

RECIPES BY CATEGORY

RECIPES BY CATEGORY

RECIPES BY CATEGORY

RECIPES BY CATEGORY